Published in 2008 by
The Original Double Red Ltd
Double Red Studios,
4 Gateway Court,
Dankerwood Road,
South Hykeham
Lincoln LN6 9UL

Tel: +44 (0)1522 693 278
www.doublered.co.uk

ISBN 978-0-9534420-4-1

Photography
James Wright
Tim Keeton
Sue Ward
Rob Hodgson
Keith Lock
Howard Boylan
David 'Chippy' Wood
David Reygondeau
All Images © Double Red

Project Manager
Sue Ward

Picture Research
Rob Hodgson

Picture Editors
James Wright
Sue Ward

Contributors
Dave Fern
Sue Jobling

Contributing Editor
Larry Carter

Design and Layout
Katie Ward
Magenta Graphics

Results and statistics
Timing Solutions Ltd. www.tsl-timing.com

Special Thanks to:
The organisers and sponsors involved in the Bennetts British Superbike Series, especially
the team at MSVR, whose dedication and commitment makes the Bennetts British
Superbike Championship the strongest domestic championship in the world. Every single
person involved in the organisation and running of the championship whose often difficult
jobs go unnoticed and unrewarded - they know who they are – the medics, physios,
marshals, press officers, journalists, television crews, truck drivers, mechanics, chefs,
cleaners, hospitality crews, commentators etc. But not least, the riders, who make the
Bennetts British Superbike Championship the amazing spectacle it is.

Contents

"You only have to do one thing to win,
and that is whatever it takes…"

Foreword
Seeing Red 2008

Winning the 2008 Bennetts British Superbike Championship means a lot to me.

I remember back at the end of last year tying up the deal with Colin Wright, I was so excited about the whole thing, almost as if this was going to be my first ever season.

I put in a lot of effort all winter long to ensure I'd be both physically and mentally strong by the time testing was due to start but then about a week or so before my first test with the team I lost my father Peter, or 'Popeye' as he was known in the Paddock, to lung cancer.

Obviously I was devastated, why my dad? He was only 67, ironically my race number, so this year was to be for him and in his memory. It started well with plenty of wins, then I had a bit of a barren patch in the middle, but ended with two wins on an amazing day at Brands Hatch, my home track. I firmly believe at the end of that first race back at Silverstone, dad was looking down and smiling. This year is for you dad, thanks for everything, Popeye!

Onwards and upwards now though, a massive thank you to everyone involved in the GSE group and Airwaves Ducati, to Petra my fiancée who's having our first child later this year, to Reggie who's been my right-hand man and a proper mate, to all my sponsors and everyone else involved in helping me in one way or another, and finally to all my fans for your unbelievable support throughout my whole career.

WSB beckons now, a similar year there next year would be nice!

Shane 'Shakey' Byrne
2008 Bennetts British Superbike Champion

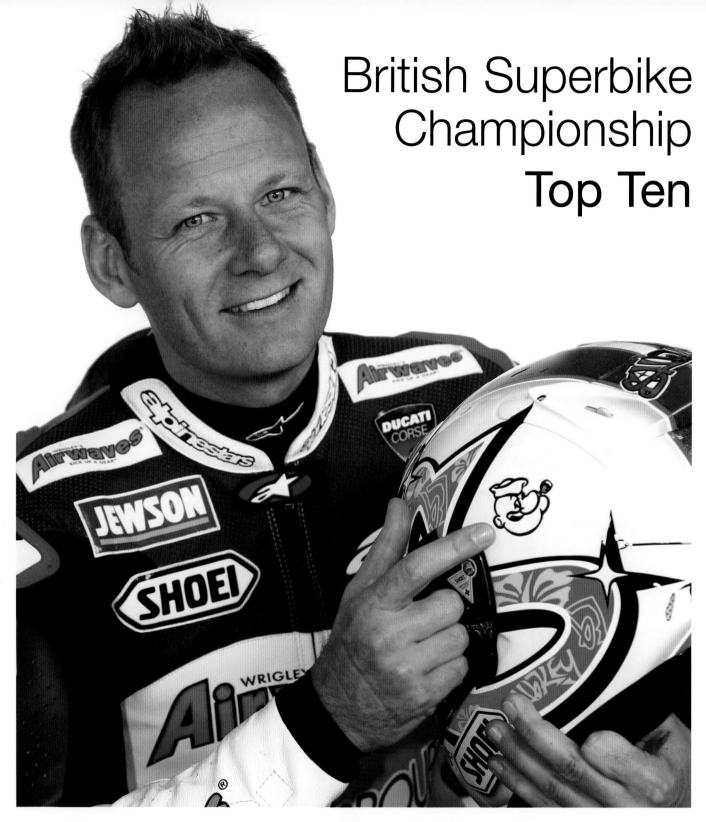

British Superbike Championship Top Ten

Results	
Position:	1
Points:	474
Poles:	5
Front Rows:	6
Best Grid:	Pole
Races:	24
Wins:	10
Podiums:	11
Best Result:	10 x 1st
Fastest Laps:	11

R1	Thruxton:	1st	+	2nd
R2	Oulton:	1st	+	1st
R3	Brands Hatch GP:	1st	+	2nd
R4	Donington:	1st	+	1st
R5	Snetterton:	2nd	+	1st
R6	Mallory:	1st	+	2nd
R7	Oulton:	3rd	+	3rd
R8	Knockhill:	2nd	+	C
R9	Cadwell:	3rd	+	3rd
R10	Croft:	5th	+	4th
R11	Silverstone:	3rd	+	2nd
R12	Brands Hatch Indy:	1st	+	1st

Shane Byrne
Airwaves Ducati

The deserved champion, who, despite not winning a race between Mallory Park in June and the final round at Brands Hatch in October really has proved to be the class of the field this season. During that lean time, he racked up the necessary points and podiums with consummate ease. In truth, it perhaps took Shakey a round longer than he would have liked to seal the deal but it really was never in doubt, despite a couple of painful slip-ups at Knockhill and Croft. With the title comes a new challenge and the news that he is moving into World Superbikes next season. He won't have chance to defend his title and as far as the British fans are concerned, he'll be sorely missed.

Leon Haslam
HM Plant Honda

Results			
Position:	2		
Points:	357		
Poles:	1		
Front Rows:	8		
Best Grid:	Pole		
Races:	24		
Wins:	5		
Podiums:	6		
Best Result:	5 x 1st		
Fastest Laps:	4		

R1	Thruxton:	4th	+	R
R2	Oulton:	2nd	+	DQ
R3	Brands Hatch GP:	4th	+	6th
R4	Donington:	2nd	+	2nd
R5	Snetterton:	5th	+	5th
R6	Mallory:	2nd	+	6th
R7	Oulton:	4th	+	4th
R8	Knockhill:	C	+	1st
R9	Cadwell:	1st	+	1st
R10	Croft:	2nd	+	1st
R11	Silverstone:	11th	+	1st
R12	Brands Hatch Indy:	4th	+	2nd

After a wretched start to the season, which only saw him score his first podium some seven races into the title chase, the second half of the season saw Haslam at his sensational best, winning five of the last nine races. Being controversially disqualified from an early race at Oulton added to Haslam's early season woes which seriously dented his title aspirations but retribution came at Silverstone when the balance was redressed with Tom Sykes. One of the toughest riders out there, as typified with him racing to a podium at the last round with an injured shoulder and collarbone, Haslam will be a big hit on the WSB stage next season with the Stiggy Honda team.

Cal Crutchlow
HM Plant Honda

Right up until mid-season, despite Byrne's dominance, Crutchlow was just to say within touching distance of the Ducati man but a combination of riding errors and a couple of machine problems saw his challenge dissipate since that early season form. Qualifying became the forte of 'The Dog' and whereas he was only off the front row once, his inability to win in the final eighteen races saw him in a battle with Sykes and Haslam for that coveted runner-up spot. Cal is moving on to the Yamaha World Supersport team for 2009 and will be a major championship contender.

Results			
Position:	3		
Points:	318		
Poles:	4		
Front Rows:	7		
Best Grid:	Pole		
Races:	24		
Wins:	2		
Podiums:	10		
Best Result:	2 x 1st		
Fastest Laps:	3		

R1	Thruxton:	2nd	+	1st
R2	Oulton:	6th	+	C
R3	Brands Hatch GP:	3rd	+	1st
R4	Donington:	6th	+	3rd
R5	Snetterton:	4th	+	3rd
R6	Mallory:	3rd	+	3rd
R7	Oulton:	6th	+	2nd
R8	Knockhill:	C	+	7th
R9	Cadwell:	5th	+	13th
R10	Croft:	4th	+	3rd
R11	Silverstone:	2nd	+	R
R12	Brands Hatch Indy:	2nd	+	4th

Tom Sykes
Rizla Suzuki

Results			
Position:	4		
Points:	316		
Poles:	2		
Front Rows:	3		
Best Grid:	Pole		
Races:	24		
Wins:	3		
Podiums:	8		
Best Result:	3 x 1st		
Fastest Laps:	4		

R1	Thruxton:	6th	+	8th
R2	Oulton:	5th	+	C
R3	Brands Hatch GP:	2nd	+	C
R4	Donington:	3rd	+	6th
R5	Snetterton:	3rd	+	7th
R6	Mallory:	4th	+	4th
R7	Oulton:	1st	+	1st
R8	Knockhill:	1st	+	4th
R9	Cadwell:	2nd	+	2nd
R10	Croft:	3rd	+	2nd
R11	Silverstone:	DQ	+	3rd
R12	Brands Hatch Indy:	6th	+	R

'The Grinner' shot to prominence courtesy of a run of victories which started with the famous and inaugural Oulton Park double in mid-season and continued at Knockhill, but his challenge for runner-up spot was flawed when he was excluded for colliding with Haslam at Silverstone and then a lacklustre final round at Brands saw him retire from race two. Blinding pace coupled with some high speed crashes were the order of the day for the ever-smiling Yorkshireman on his high-revving Suzuki in the early part of this season, otherwise he'd have been a major contender for the title. But bigger fish to fry have come his way with his ride in WSB with the factory Yamaha team next season.

Leon Camier
Airwaves Ducati

Results	
Position:	5
Points:	306
Poles:	0
Front Rows:	1
Best Grid:	3rd
Races:	22
Wins:	3
Podiums:	5
Best Result:	3 x 1st
Fastest Laps:	1

R1	Thruxton:	5th	+	4th
R2	Oulton:	3rd	+	3rd
R3	Brands Hatch GP:	5th	+	3rd
R4	Donington:	5th	+	4th
R5	Snetterton:	1st	+	2nd
R6	Mallory:	C	+	8th
R7	Oulton:	NS	+	NS
R8	Knockhill:	5th	+	8th
R9	Cadwell:	4th	+	4th
R10	Croft:	1st	+	5th
R11	Silverstone:	1st	+	4th
R12	Brands Hatch Indy:	5th	+	3rd

After a superb debut win at Snetterton, which moved him into second behind his team-mate, it seemed as if Camier would go on to take the challenge to Byrne but then came Mallory and a high-speed tumble in race one which was followed by him having to sit out both Oulton races after a crash during qualifying. Since then, 'The Shafter' really came of age, racking up back-to-back wins at Croft and Silverstone before rounding the season off on the podium at Brands. With the Gang of Four leaving for pastures new, it really could be Camier's turn to win the title in BSB next term.

Michael Rutter
NW200 Ducati

Back with Ducati, Rutter started the season strongly with a double podium at Thruxton before fading in subsequent meetings, but then the fairytale happened. Riding at his local track at Mallory, 'The Blade' defied a bruising race one crash to sensationally take his first victory in three long years, and when added to his North West 200 success, this season turned out to be one to remember for the veteran! He was on the podium in mixed conditions at Knockhill and celebrated his three-hundredth BSB start in the final round at Brands in October. He's coming back for more next season and is still as hungry as ever to land that elusive first-ever BSB crown.

Results	
Position:	6
Points:	256
Poles:	0
Front Rows:	5
Best Grid:	2nd
Races:	24
Wins:	1
Podiums:	3
Best Result:	1 x 1st
Fastest Laps:	0

R1	Thruxton:	3rd	+	3rd
R2	Oulton:	4th	+	6th
R3	Brands Hatch GP:	C	+	5th
R4	Donington:	8th	+	8th
R5	Snetterton:	9th	+	4th
R6	Mallory:	C	+	1st
R7	Oulton:	7th	+	11th
R8	Knockhill:	4th	+	2nd
R9	Cadwell:	6th	+	5th
R10	Croft:	6th	+	6th
R11	Silverstone:	4th	+	7th
R12	Brands Hatch Indy:	7th	+	6th

James Ellison
Hydrex Bike Animal Honda

Results	
Position:	7
Points:	230
Poles:	0
Front Rows:	1
Best Grid:	2nd
Races:	22
Wins:	0
Podiums:	4
Best Result:	2 x 2nd
Fastest Laps:	0

R1	Thruxton:	7th	+	7th
R2	Oulton:	8th	+	2nd
R3	Brands Hatch GP:	6th	+	8th
R4	Donington:	4th	+	5th
R5	Snetterton:	7th	+	10th
R6	Mallory:	5th	+	11th
R7	Oulton:	2nd	+	5th
R8	Knockhill:	3rd	+	5th
R9	Cadwell:	NS	+	NS
R10	Croft:	9th	+	7th
R11	Silverstone:	C	+	6th
R12	Brands Hatch Indy:	3rd	+	5th

One of the surprise packages of the season, the former MotoGP rider shot back to prominence with some scintillating performances despite him and his team getting to grips with the Honda and familiarising himself with the circuits after three years away. A training injury ruled him out of Cadwell but such was the consistency of bike and rider, it was only a crash at Silverstone that wrecked Ellison's 100% finishing record. The only thing missing from an impressive repertoire this year was a race victory but that will come next season, and with it, quite possibly the championship as the amiable Cumbrian is set to join Leon Camier at the GSE Yamaha team.

Simon Andrews
Lloyds British Yamaha

It took until Donington Park at round four before the enigmatic Andrews squeezed into the top ten with his first double score of the season, having posted points, albeit good ones, in just 50% of the previous races. But it was at Mallory at the half way stage that he really started to score strongly and since then 'Trip' was never outside the top ten in the following twelve races demonstrating incredible consistency and in doing so, became top Yamaha rider in the series. A seriously underestimated class act who is surely destined to challenge for the title next season.

Results	
Position:	8
Points:	176
Poles:	0
Front Rows:	0
Best Grid:	6th
Races:	24
Wins:	0
Podiums:	0
Best Result:	2 x 5th
Fastest Laps:	0

R1	Thruxton:	8th +	R
R2	Oulton:	C +	7th
R3	Brands Hatch GP:	9th +	R
R4	Donington:	10th +	9th
R5	Snetterton:	10th +	8th
R6	Mallory:	7th +	7th
R7	Oulton:	5th +	6th
R8	Knockhill:	8th +	6th
R9	Cadwell:	7th +	6th
R10	Croft:	10th +	9th
R11	Silverstone:	5th +	8th
R12	Brands Hatch Indy:	8th +	7th

Michael Laverty
Relentless Suzuki by TAS

Results	
Position:	9
Points:	141
Poles:	0
Front Rows:	2
Best Grid:	2nd
Races:	24
Wins:	0
Podiums:	0
Best Result:	2 x 4th
Fastest Laps:	1

R1	Thruxton:	10th +	5th
R2	Oulton:	7th +	4th
R3	Brands Hatch GP:	C +	4th
R4	Donington:	9th +	R
R5	Snetterton:	6th +	6th
R6	Mallory:	11th +	C
R7	Oulton:	9th +	7th
R8	Knockhill:	6th +	R
R9	Cadwell:	8th +	9th
R10	Croft:	7th +	10th
R11	Silverstone:	C +	15th
R12	Brands Hatch Indy:	R +	R

Just one measly point from his last four races typified 'Choo-Choo's' season which promised so very much and in reality delivered very little. On his return to the BSB class after winning the Supersport title in 2007, the young Ulsterman was so close to the podium on a few occasions and also at the cutting edge during qualifying. The TAS Suzuki was competitive as Laverty has proved by leading both races at Mallory. He was foiled by the weather with incorrect tyre choices on a couple of occasions, and found himself tangled up with other people's crashes on others. A former podium finisher in BSB, Michael will bounce back bigger and stronger in 2009.

Tristan Palmer
Tena For Men Honda

After winning last year's BSB privateer's title, Palmer's ascension into the works ranks was truly amazing and having scored points in all bar one race, his presence inside the top ten is justified. On the ex Greg Lavilla Honda Fireblade, Palmer was a regular thorn in the sides of the fancied BSB front runners, as highlighted by his superb sixth position at Silverstone. A rider with considerable BSB experience, the Midlander goes about his racing in a quiet yet professional manner and the fact that the likes of Harris, McConnell, Easton, Watanabe and Smart finished behind him speaks volumes about his ability.

Results	
Position:	10
Points:	111
Poles:	0
Front Rows:	0
Best Grid:	8th
Races:	24
Wins:	0
Podiums:	0
Best Result:	6th
Fastest Laps:	0

R1	Thruxton:	13th +	13th
R2	Oulton:	9th +	11th
R3	Brands Hatch GP:	10th +	11th
R4	Donington:	12th +	14th
R5	Snetterton:	13th +	9th
R6	Mallory:	8th +	9th
R7	Oulton:	C +	12th
R8	Knockhill:	9th +	12th
R9	Cadwell:	11th +	12th
R10	Croft:	14th +	14th
R11	Silverstone:	6th +	12th
R12	Brands Hatch Indy:	10th +	13th

Airwaves Ducati

Airwaves Ducati

Machinery: Ducati 1098R F08
Manager: Colin Wright
Located: Ashford, Kent
Pedigree: British Superbike Champions 1999, 2000, 2005 & 2008

With the departure of long-term riders Gregorio Lavilla and Leon Haslam last year, this was a team with a brand new line up at the start of 2008, with former champion Shane 'Shakey' Byrne and promising youngster Leon Camier aboard the evolutionary 1200cc versions of the 1098 Ducatis.

After guiding such luminaries as British Champions Troy Bayliss and Neil Hodgson in their colours, as well as James Toseland, onto the World Superbike stage, the team eventually returned to BSB and promptly won the title in 2005 with Greg Lavilla.

Byrne won his first British title on Ducati machinery back in 2003 and after a season of domination this year, particularly in the first half, Byrne added his second crown and GSE Racing's fourth after a late season stutter which included big crashes at Knockhill and then Croft, to box off the title a round early at Silverstone.

Camier has also come of age this season and as well as taking three wins, including two in the final three rounds, he has been a regular podium finisher and but for a poor mid-season run which included a big off at Mallory and also ruling himself out of Oulton, he'd have been a strong contender to make it an Airwaves Ducati one-two.

But the shock news that greeted the paddock towards the end of the season was that the team would be switching allegiances from Ducati for 2009, with whom they enjoyed a ten-year relationship, to Yamaha in a three-year deal to race in BSB.

Riders:

Shane Byrne		Leon Camier	
Number:	67	Number:	2
DOB:	10 December, 1976	DOB:	4 August, 1986
Lives:	Zurich, Switzerland	Lives:	Wimborne, Dorset
Races:	171	Races:	44
Wins:	27	Wins:	3
2008 Position:	1st	2008 Position:	5th

HM Plant
Honda
Racing

HM Plant Honda

Machinery: Honda CBR1000RR Fireblade
Manager: Havier Beltran
Located: Louth, Lincolnshire
Pedigree: British Superbike Champions 2006 & 2007

With double champion Ryuichi Kiyonari and sidekick Jonathan Rea departing to the World Superbike paddock at the end of last season, the defending champions also recruited a pair of new riders to take up the cudgels in the quest for the hat-trick.

Aboard the new 2008 specification HM Plant sponsored Fireblades, young-guns Leon Haslam and Cal Crutchlow started the season amongst the favourites, especially as both had enjoyed success on Honda machinery in the past.

The team was without the factory HRC parts and trick Michelin tyres this year, but otherwise the nucleus of this very experienced team, some of whom won World titles in WSB with Colin Edwards, remained the same.

Despite starting the season strongly, Crutchlow didn't enjoy the best of fortunes and whereas once he was in with a shout of challenging Shakey Byrne for the title, his challenge faded as the season progressed. Conversely, it took seven races for Haslam to record his first podium finish but towards the end of the season, he became the man to beat with a string of victories as he moved clear into second place in the championship.

It turned out to be a one-year tenure for both riders as both Crutchlow, who announced his plans to move into the World Supersport arena for 2009, and Haslam who is moving into World Superbikes, departed the Louth-based team at the end of the season.

Riders:

Leon Haslam		Cal Crutchlow	
Number:	91	Number:	35
DOB:	31 May, 1983	DOB:	27 October, 1985
Lives:	Smalley, Derbyshire	Lives:	Coventry, Warwickshire
Races:	113	Races:	50
Wins:	16	Wins:	2
2008 Position:	2nd	2008 Position:	3rd

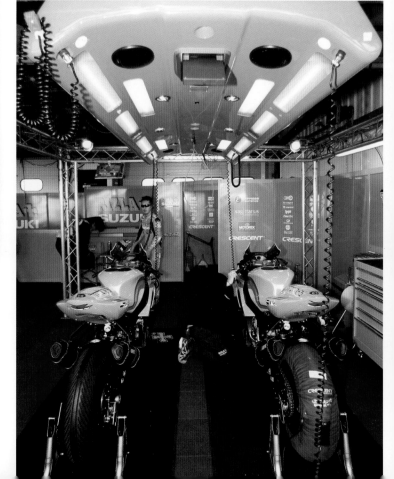

Rizla Suzuki

Machinery: Suzuki GSX-R1000 K8
Manager: Jack Valentine
Located: Verwood, Dorset
Pedigree: British Superbike Champions 2004

Another season of change for the official Suzuki representatives with Japanese rookie Atsushi Watanabe lining up alongside the talented Tom Sykes and a new Team Manager in the shape of the successful and experienced Jack Valentine.

Watanabe came to the UK as the reigning All-Japan Superbike Champion and was sent over to do a job, presumably similar to what fellow-countryman Kiyonari did twice for Honda. Sykes returned to the make of bike on which he made his name in British Supersport, prior to a debut BSB season on a Honda last year, where he was so impressive. Sykes also made his BSB debut on a Rizla bike when deputising for the injured Yukio Kagayama in 2003.

However, the amiable Japanese rider really failed to cut the mustard this season and languished well down the order in the championship with only one top seven placing to his name whereas Sykes has simply been a revelation.

Enjoying their seventh and final year of backing from Rizla, Sykes had a couple of big crashes early in the season, namely at Thruxton and Brands, but from the mid-point onwards, the Yorkshireman really has got to grips with the bike and became a major force as the season progressed. Notwithstanding his exclusion from the opening race at Silverstone in the penultimate round, when he took out Leon Haslam, 'The Grinner' finished on the podium in all but three of his last twelve races, including standing on the top step on three of those occasions.

Tom Sykes

Number:	66
DOB:	19 August, 1985
Lives:	Huddersfield, West Yorkshire
Races:	52
Wins:	3
2008 Position:	4th

Atsushi Watanabe

Number:	14
DOB:	22 September, 1976
Lives:	Hammamatsu, Japan / Bournemouth, Dorset
Races:	24
Wins:	0
2008 Position:	14th

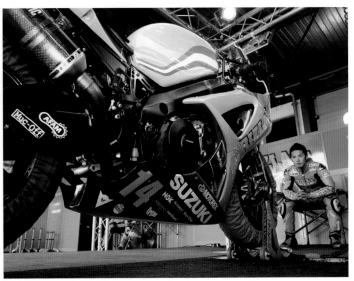

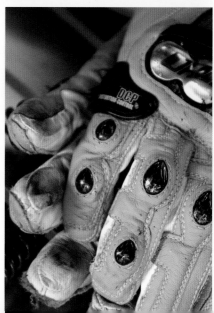

NW200 Ducati

NW200 Ducati

Machinery: Ducati 1098R
Owner: John Hackett
Located: Coventry, Warwickshire
Pedigree: British Superbike Cup Champions & NW200
Race Winners

The JH Performance Racing Team was this year backed by Alistair and Adele Kennedy, who also sponsor the North West 200. They teamed up with multiple winner Michael Rutter as part of the promotion of the great Irish road race which took place in May with Rutter recording his twelfth win.

Armed with the latest Ducati machinery, Rutter bounced back after a couple of poor seasons, including 2007 where he was injured for much of the year. However, after a promising start to the season with a double podium at Thruxton, 'The Blade' tailed off a little, but then came Mallory Park where he took a sensational win in yet another weather-affected race which has been so typical of the last two seasons.   Since then, Rutter was the model of consistency posting a string of top six placings, including another podium at Knockhill and being a regular front row qualifier.

Also drafted into the team this year was Ulsterman John Laverty, who originally planned to contest the National Superstock Championship. He ultimately joined Rutter in BSB on the Buildbase-backed 1098 Ducati, and after comfortably leading the Daily Star Superbike Cup, despite missing out at Knockhill where he was injured during practice, he bounced back to land the title at Croft with two rounds in-hand.

Riders:

Michael Rutter		John Laverty (P)	
Number:	200	Number:	201
DOB:	18 April, 1973	DOB:	6 July, 1982
Lives:	Bridgnorth, Shropshire	Lives:	Toomebridge, Northern Ireland
Races:	301	Races:	38
Wins:	26	Wins:	0
2008 Position:	6th	2008 Position:	17th

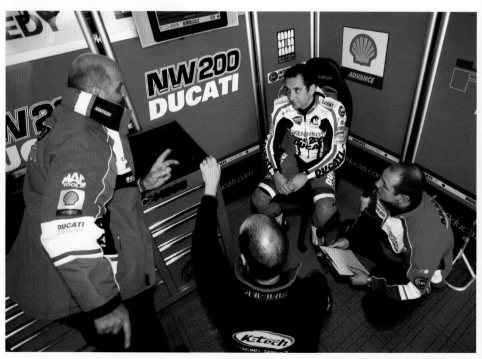

Pit Wall

MSS Discovery
Kawasaki

MSS Discovery Kawasaki

Machinery: Kawasaki ZX10-R
Owners: Nick Morgan and Stuart Simmonds
Located: Thorpe-le-Soken, Essex
Pedigree: British Supersport Race Winners

The amalgamation of the two teams continued into 2008 and after last season which saw the official Kawasaki UK-backed team in the doldrums, lessons were learnt and they came back for another stab at BSB with two riders with a proven pedigree, albeit not necessarily in Superbikes.

Scotsman Stuart Easton was a former British Supersport Champion who has flirted with the big bikes although his career of late has been dogged by injury and Aussie Billy McConnell won the Virgin Media Cup a couple of seasons back and returned to BSB after a year in BSS.

A combination of the raw talent that these two possess, coupled with their experience on Pirelli rubber, when combined with the new rules which were designed to help teams such as this, saw them spring the odd surprise this season.

Easton showed a lot of promise with a pair of solid top tens at Thruxton and a fifth at Oulton but a high-speed crash in practice at Snetterton saw him ruled out with injury for a number of rounds. 'Skippy' was also well inside the points in the opening races and despite having just one bike each, the pair have shown great consistency with a string of fantastic rides.

Despite McConnell having a nightmare at Croft, the pair started to string a few decent results together at the end of the season, especially at Silverstone when they posted a top ten finish apiece.

Riders:

Billy McConnell		**Stuart Easton**	
Number:	8	Number:	3
DOB:	24 December, 1986	DOB:	21 July, 1984
Lives:	Adelaide, Australia	Lives:	Hawick, Scotland
	Hinckley, Leicestershire	Races:	28
Races:	46	Wins:	0
Wins:	0	2008 Position:	13th
2008 Position:	12th		

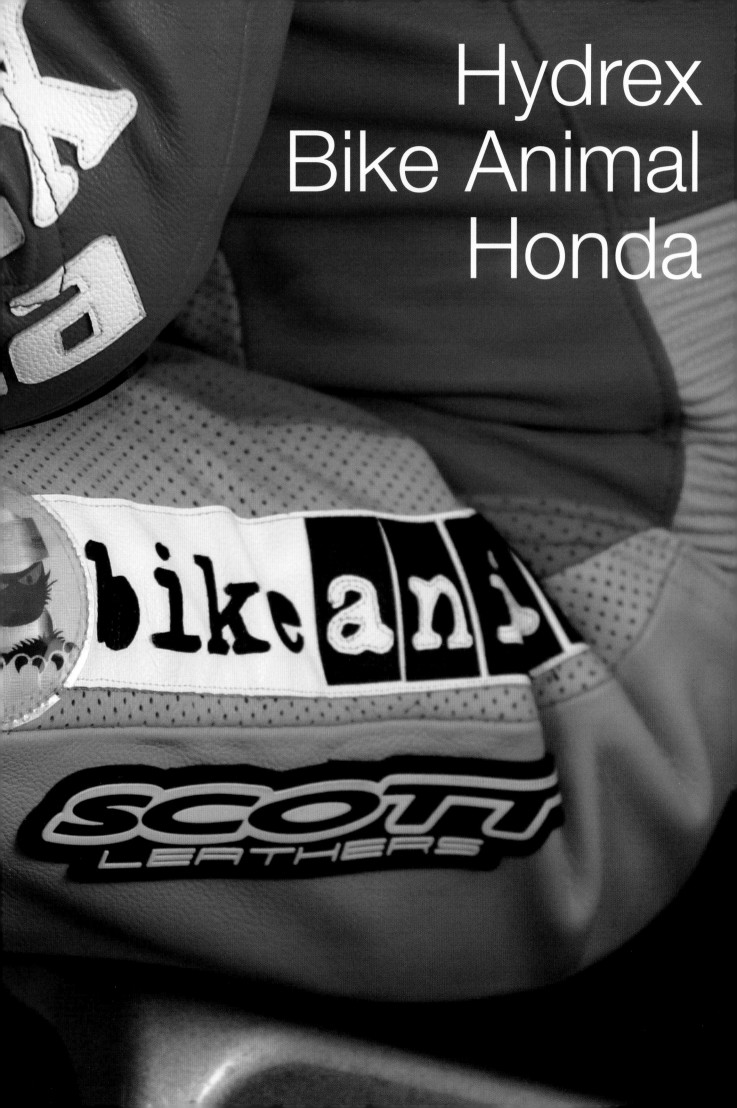

Hydrex
Bike Animal
Honda

Hydrex Bike Animal Honda

Machinery: Honda CBR1000RR Fireblade
Owner: Shaun Muir
Located: Guisborough, Cleveland
Pedigree: Podium finishers in BSB, NW200 & TT, Ulster GP winners

After a couple of difficult years, Shaun Muir's team returned bigger and stronger with a concerted effort to bid for 2008 honours.

Joining long-term sponsors Hydrex was the biker's website Bike Animal and alongside the charismatic Guy Martin, returned the former MotoGP and AMA Superbike rider James Ellison. Martin has gained an awesome reputation on the closed roads whereas Ellison, the 2004 Superbike Cup Champion, ex World Endurance Champion and double European Superstock Champion, added to his impressive CV in his first full BSB season in four years.

Martin, with his mutton chop sideburns, and Ellison, the pin-up with the boy-band looks, both proved to be massive hits with the fans again this year, both on and off the track, and with the latest 2008 Fireblades in their arsenal, with good reason.

Despite early season handling problems and not seeing many of the tracks in four long years, Ellison was the surprise package of the season what with four podiums in total and his ability to run at the front. His coup de grace, however, was a simply stunning performance as a wild card at the WSB meeting at Donington when he qualified as top Brit and finished a battling fourth in one of the races.

In contrast, Martin really struggled with the bike this season, leading to a number of non-finishes but recorded podium finishes at the NW200 and TT. He also won at the Southern 100 before taking a record-breaking sixth win at the Scarborough Gold Cup.

Riders:

James Ellison		**Guy Martin**	
Number:	7	Number:	9
DOB:	19 September, 1980	DOB:	4 November, 1981
Lives:	Kendal, Cumbria	Lives:	Kirmington, North Lincolnshire
Races:	48	Races:	34
Wins:	0	Wins:	0
2008 Position:	7th	2008 Position:	18th

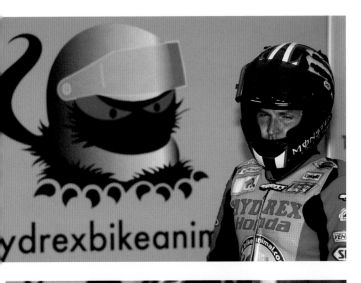

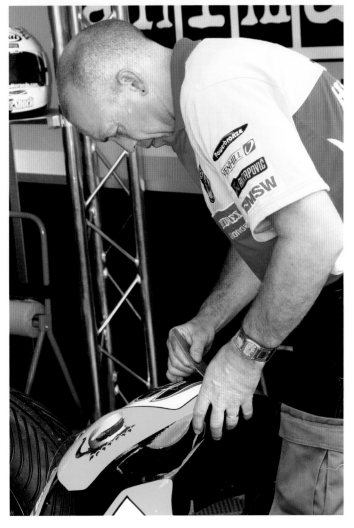

Relentless Suzuki

Machinery: Suzuki GSX-R1000 K8
Manager: Phillip Neill
Located: Moneymore, Northern Ireland
Pedigree: British Supersport Champions 2007

After finishing 1-2 in last year's British Supersport Championship, the Ulster-based TAS team moved into BSB for 2008 as a single rider team although they are very experienced in running such bikes as their road racing history at the TT, NW200 and Ulster GP testifies.

Although aged only 26, Michael Laverty has plenty of British Superbike experience and was a rostrum finisher a couple of seasons ago and so it proved again in 2008 as he was again at the cutting edge of both qualifying and in the racing.

Having led some races and front-running in plenty of others, Laverty, who has also tested the tarmac a few times, some of his own making but quite often not, just missed out on the podium three times this season, following up a fifth at Thruxton with fourth place finishes at both Oulton Park and Brands.

Mechanical problems, mainly to do with the clutch, meant Laverty didn't finish the final couple of races but for the team which gained a double win at the TT and podium placings at the NW200, it was valuable experience gained as they look to improve in 2009.

Rider:

Michael Laverty

Number:	4
DOB:	7 June, 1981
Lives:	Toomebridge, Northern Ireland
Races:	67
Wins:	0
2008 Position:	9th

R M Yamaha

Machinery: Yamaha YZF R1
Owner: Rob McElnea
Located: Scunthorpe, North Lincolnshire
Pedigree: British Superbike Champions 1996, 1997 & 1998

Ten years after their last BSB crown with Niall Mackenzie, ex GP racer Rob McElnea whittled his squad down considerably for 2008 with multiple British Supersport Champion Karl Harris being the sole rider this season.

In the guise of Virgin Yamaha for many years, McElnea's team switched to Pirelli tyres three seasons ago so they had a bit of a jump on their rivals on the Italian rubber and with all of Harris' major successes coming as a single rider, it should have been the recipe for some overdue success.

However, the Gods conspired to such a degree that it took until round four at Donington for 'The Bomber' to chalk his first points up on the board after an injury ravaged start to the season which saw him sit the rescheduled round at Brands out following that high-speed smash at Thruxton. But for 'arm-pump' due to not muscling the bike around for a few weeks, it could have been a podium at Donington and more woes saw him DNF in races at Snetterton and Mallory before that controversial clash with Shakey Byrne at Oulton which had the team bosses arguing the toss on live TV!

With the one high spot being the deserved podium at Knockhill, it really has been a season of what might have been for the fan's favourite who was looking good at the final round at Brands before having to leave the track prematurely without racing due to a domestic problem.

Rider:

Karl Harris
Number:	5
DOB:	21 October, 1979
Lives:	Sheffield, Yorkshire
Races:	111
Wins:	0
2008 Position:	11th

SMT Honda

Machinery: Honda CBR1000RR Fireblade
Owner: Robin Croft
Located: Skelmersdale, Lancashire
Pedigree: Points scorers in BSB

After a debut season last year when they chose to contest the main BSB Championship instead of the Superbike Cup with rider Aaron Zanotti, they were regular points scorers and indeed have enjoyed plenty of success in the support classes in recent years.

Rider Adam Jenkinson, the former minimoto champion, looked to be a rising star who was a regular podium finisher in the Virgin Cup and National Superstock Championships in recent times. However, after a stunning performance in qualifying and in race one at Thruxton, Jenkinson crashed at high speed and sustained injuries which kept him out for the rest of the season.

Subsequently, the team drafted in various riders as deputies including Sean Emmett and Marshall Neill as well as Superbike rookie Tom Grant, who was doing a great job until he crashed, through no fault of his own, at Knockhill and suffered a serious arm injury meaning he too was placed on the sick list!

Croft saw the introduction of Australian Supersport Champion, Jason O'Halloran, who proceeded to be singularly impressive. His eighth place at Silverstone and strong performance in the final round at Brands proved to be the tonic the team had been sadly missing.

Rider:

Jason O'Halloran

Number:	22
DOB:	30 December, 1987
Lives:	Wollongong, Australia
Races:	6
Wins:	0
2008 Position:	19th

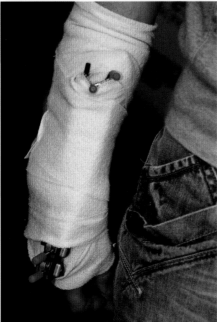

Tena for Men

Machinery: Honda CBR1000RR Fireblade
Owner: Darrell Halstead
Located: Burnley, Lancashire
Pedigree: British Superbike Cup Champions 2007

Incorporating former professional rugby league player, Michael Howarth's Team Howie Racing outfit (THR), which started last season in unfortunate style with Howarth crashing in morning warm up for the very first round and ruling himself out for the season with a broken leg! They drafted in ex BSB racer Tristan Palmer as a replacement who, despite missing the opening couple of rounds whilst racing in the USA, promptly netted the 2007 BSB Cup as top privateer meaning all's well that ended well for the team!

Howarth came back for another season, albeit running in the Superbike Cup class with Palmer, rather unsurprisingly for those fans who know him, running inside the top ten in the overall standings, with a string of top names behind him.

Scoring in every race bar one indiscretion at Oulton, Palmer's best result came at Silverstone when he roared to a sixth place finish as well as a great performance at his local track of Mallory Park where he ran at the front for a while before netting himself a pair of top ten finishes.

As for Howarth, his season was badly disrupted by injury, the latest of which saw him break his collarbone at Croft and then an industrial accident the week before the Brands finale ruled him out with broken ribs.

Riders:

Tristan Palmer		**Michael Howarth (P)**	
Number:	33	Number:	27
DOB:	17 August, 1982	DOB:	4 October, 1977
Lives:	New Arley, Warwickshire	Lives:	Burnley, Lancashire
Races:	72	Races:	34
Wins:	0	Wins:	0
2008 Position:	10th	2008 Position:	N/A

Hawk Kawasaki

Machinery: Kawasaki ZX10-R
Owner: Stuart Hicken
Located: Peggs Green, Leicestershire
Pedigree: Race winners in BSB

Bucking the trend of all-new teams, Stuart Hicken's squad was planning on returning with both riders who finished the 2007 season with them in the shape of the vastly experienced duo of James Haydon and Scott Smart.

However, budgetary constraints decreed that only one rider in the shape of Smart could be in action for the team with Haydon waiting in the wings should sponsorship be forthcoming.

Injuries and poor performances by certain riders haven't helped their cause in recent seasons but with consistency coupled with experience for 2008, it started to come together once again for the Hawk squad. Who will ever forget Smart's crowning glory for the team, when he beat a stunned John Reynolds to the line at Mondello four seasons ago to record his and the team's debut victory and in doing so, the first victory for the ZX10-R anywhere in the world.

After steadily improving in the opening few rounds, Smart's results dried up in mid-season before getting back on the points trail. Smart was certainly a rider to watch when the weather turned wet and with another summer of inclement conditions, Smarty had a handful of top ten finishes but they were not quite the results that either he or the team were looking for.

Rider:

Scott Smart

Number:	88
DOB:	29 May, 1975
Lives:	Maidstone, Kent
Races:	140
Wins:	4
2008 Position:	15th

Team Maxxis

Machinery: Honda CBR1000RR Fireblade
Owner: John Jameson
Located: Liverpool
Pedigree: British Superbike Cup Champions 2006

Having won the British Superbike Cup in 2006 with Chris Martin, the team underwent several rider changes last year before settling with the venerable Australian David Johnson who rode for them once again.

'The Aussie DJ' is a class act who has chased rides for the past few seasons and has a winning pedigree but now with a permanent ride, he has been able to demonstrate his talent further and, but for some reliability issues, Johnson would have been much higher up the points table than he eventually finished.

An injured wrist, courtesy of a training accident, hampered his bid towards the end of the season but to end up just outside the top twenty in the tightest domestic championship of its kind in the world is no mean achievement!

Rider:

David Johnson

Number:	68
DOB:	16 April, 1982
Lives:	Adelaide, Australia / Hinckley Leicestershire
Races:	38
Wins:	0
2008 Position:	21st

Lloyds British Yamaha

Machinery: Yamaha YZF-R1
Owner: Bernie Toleman
Located: Quedgeley, Gloucestershire
Pedigree: British Superbike Cup Champions 2004

The enigmatic Simon Andrews rode for the team that won the Superbike Cup in 2004 with James Ellison and judging by his occasional flash of brilliance over the past couple of seasons, Bernie Toleman's boys had every chance of sampling the champagne again this season.

Despite missing some races mid-season last year due to budget constraints and injuries, the team racked up some good results and with their previous experience on Pirelli tyres, they proved this season that they are as quick as many of their rivals.

As ever, Andrews once again proved to be very rapid as well as being top Yamaha rider in the series. Such has been his and the team's consistency, he has only failed to reach the top ten on three occasions throughout the whole season, which in itself is a remarkable feat.

The highlight was at a dry Silverstone whereby Andrews claimed an impressive fifth position to add to the similar placing he scored in the wet at Oulton Park earlier in the season.

Rider:

Simon Andrews

Number:	17
DOB:	14 August, 1983
Lives:	Evesham, Worcestershire
Races:	50
Wins:	0
2008 Position:	8th

Red Viper Racing

Machinery: Honda CBR1000RR Fireblade
Owner: Ady Butterworth
Located: Warrington, Cheshire
Pedigree: Points Scorers in BSB

Having formed the team at the start of 2007, Ady Butterworth and his crew had a valuable year of experience under their belts and finished just outside the top twenty with Chris Martin.

Former Superstock race winner Aaron Zanotti joined the team this year after a superb debut in the BSB class last season where he gained experience of Honda machinery towards the end of the year. However, after a tough season, Zanotti had a big crash at Croft meaning he was ruled out of Silverstone and Brands allowing youngster Peter Hickman to take over the ride. Hickman managed a point on his debut, and just missed out in the final races at Brands.

Rider:

Peter Hickman

Number:	60
DOB:	8 April, 1987
Lives:	Alford, Lincolnshire
Races:	43
Wins:	0
2008 Position:	33rd

THE ROAD TO VICTORY

Critically-acclaimed Triple Tread Compound technology

» Victory and fastest lap in the 2008 Isle of Man TT Senior race with John McGuinness
» Victory in the 2008 Isle of Man TT Supersport race with Steve Plater
» A hat-trick of wins and new Supersport lap record at the North West 200 with Steve Plater
» Race-bred technology now available for the street
» True technology transfer

"DUNLOP'S TRIPLE TREAD COMPOUND TECHNOLOGY GIVES ME THE CONFIDENCE TO PUSH MYSELF TO THE LIMIT AT THE ISLE OF MAN TT. I FEEL INCREDIBLY LOYAL TO DUNLOP AS IN 2008 THEY ONCE AGAIN HELPED ME TO VICTORY." John McGuinness

THE SPORTMAX FAMILY

TTC
» GRIP
» FEEL
» CONTROL
» TRIPLE TREAD COMPOUND »

» **www.dunlopmotorcycle.co.uk** » GP Racer Slick » GP Racer » Qualifier RR » Qualifier D209 » Roadsmart

Brands Hatch GP

6th April

Left: How much snow?

Below: The only person having any fun at Brands was James Toseland - in the company of the Bennetts grid girls

Brands Hatch GP
6th April

SNOW JOKE...

For the first time in living memory, the opening round of the Bennetts British Superbike Championship was postponed due to heavy snowfall on race day morning. However, some quick work by the organisers meant that they were able to revise the date for the following month rather than lose the round altogether.

So, when not involved in snowball fights or building snowmen, everyone packed up and went home early!

THINK! UNIT HOSTS BSB STARS

The THINK! road safety campaign has been a major sponsor of the Bennetts British Superbike Championship for five years now and the interactive unit, which visited every round, has firmly established itself as one of the series' most popular and engaging features.

The specially designed unit gives riders expert advice from industry specialists and has the main messages 'Save Racing for the Track' and 'Give your Bike the Skills it Deserves'. With regular BSB interviews, all the latest Superbikes on hand, competitions, giveaways, a riding simulator and interactive computers, the Academy is a fun and entertaining way to learn more about staying safe on the road.

2008 rider guests included James Toseland, newly crowned British Superbike Champion Shane Byrne and fellow protagonists Leon Haslam, Tom Sykes, Cal Crutchlow, Michael Rutter plus regular interviewees THINK! Ambassador John Reynolds and Niall Mackenzie.

Visit the THINK! Motorcycle Academy online at www.dft.gov.uk/thinkmotorcycleacademy

BSB riders assemble at Snetterton

Toseland addresses the fans at the THINK! unit

Rider signing session at Brands Hatch

The THINK! Motorcycle Academy at Silverstone

The THINK! Campaign would like to thank its loyal partners for their ongoing support.

Thruxton

20th April

Top: In what was effectively the opening round, Leon Haslam contemplates the season ahead

Above: Rizla's new boy from Japan, Atsushi Watanabe received support from former BSB star, Yukio Kagayama

Left: Cal gets on the gas

Right: Tom Sykes' Rizla Suzuki snakes around searching for grip over the Thruxton bumps

Below: The man at the top of BSB, Jonathan Palmer, chats with Shakey Byrne on the grid - probably about cameras or helicopters!

Thruxton
20th April

SHAKEY AND CAL SHARE THE OPENING SPOILS...

After the snow-bound Brands Hatch meeting was postponed, Shane 'Shakey' Byrne began his bid to regain the crown he last held in 2003 with victory first time out aboard the Airwaves Ducati, however, he had to settle for second best in race two as Cal Crutchlow, riding the HM Plant Honda, chalked up his first ever success in the top flight.

Behind them in each race was the rejuvenated Michael Rutter, enjoying his best day at the races for some time. Taking a pair of thirds aboard the North West 200 Ducati the elder statesman of the series enthused: "It's a mega feeling to be back up front and it has been a long time coming."

Crutchlow had set a hot pace in the opener at this high-speed, bumpy circuit, leading a Superbike race for the first time since his graduation a year earlier with his team-mate Leon Haslam also in the frame, but pole-starter Byrne nosed ahead at Seagrave to take the victory.

The tables were turned next time out, though not before a frightening incident in which Karl Harris took the full force of Tom Sykes' flying Rizla Suzuki across the front of his helmet at around 120mph. Sykes, thrown off a split second earlier hurt his thumb, while Harris, who joked that he looked more like a boxer coming out of the ring than a racer, took a heavy bruising.

Sykes made the re-start of the race but was soon overtaken by Crutchlow who was in no mood to let anyone deny him the victor's champagne, riding in a strong and determined fashion he held off Byrne by a couple of seconds at the chequered flag.

"Shakey kept me honest in the first race but next time out I managed to get away and kept a pretty consistent gap. There's more of this to come" reflected Crutchlow who ended the meeting as joint leader of the series with Byrne - each on 45 points.

Haslam, fourth in the opener, stopped with a technical problem early on in the second race while Leon Camier racked up solid points with fifth and fourth places. In the Daily Star Cup John Laverty rode the Buildbase NW200 Ducati to a winning double.

BSB Championship Positions			**Cup Championship Positions**		
1	BYRNE	45	1	J LAVERTY	50
2	CRUTCHLOW	45	2	JESSOPP	30
3	RUTTER	32	3	ASHLEY	29
4	CAMIER	24	4	BUCKINGHAM	22
5	SYKES	18	5	TUNSTALL	22
6	ELLISON	18	6	BURNS	20

Rivetted

GLEN RICHARDS
British Supersport
Champion 2008

TSUBAKI
Chain with in-built
Japanese reliability.

Oulton Park

5th May

Below left: MotoGP star Marco Melandri catches up with former classmate James Ellison

Above left: Simon Andrews backs in his Lloyds British Yamaha at Lodge corner

Above: Tom Sykes' training came to the fore as he was forced to sprint back to the pits to collect his spare bike following a turn one melee as the rain started

Oulton Park
5th May

SHAKEY AT THE DOUBLE AS HASLAM BOOTED OUT…

S hane Byrne powered in double top amid rain, red flags, tumbles and controversy in this first visit to the Cheshire circuit, but the Airwaves Ducati rider was equal to all of the challenges, even his own mistake in the second race, as he confirmed his lead in the rankings.

The 2003 champ was showing something which even at this stage his rivals were lacking - consistency, and although both Tom Sykes and Cal Crutchlow were given a reprieve after tumbling early in a first race halted by rain, the re-start came amid tyre gambles. "The boys in the team chose the tyres for me, I just rode them pushing as hard as I could," explained Byrne.

Byrne came through from fourth, picking off first Haslam, then Sykes and was well placed to go through as the leader, Crutchlow, ran wide through the gravel at Lodge. Haslam closed the leader, Byrne, down, but could not catch him, taking second ahead of Leon Camier, Michael Rutter and Tom Sykes.

There was more bad luck for Karl Harris who had cut off his own plaster cast on the foot injured at Thruxton to race, only to crash in the early stages.

Sykes led next time out from Crutchlow and Haslam while Byrne was playing a self enforced game of catch up in a race that saw the determined Haslam excluded from the results after race officials deemed his overtaking move that sent Sykes tumbling out at Hizzy's, to have been careless.

Starting from pole, Crutchlow held the upper hand, but Byrne took him on the twelfth lap, and next time round Crutchlow crashed heavily at Druids sustaining ankle injuries. Victory, for the third time in four races, went to Byrne with the impressive James Ellison bringing his Hydrex Bike Animal Honda into second place while Leon Camier completed a pair of thirds to take second place in the Championship standings behind his team-mate Byrne.

Steve Mercer took the Daily Star Cup honours in the first race, ahead of Chris Burns but John Laverty, sixth in race one, was back to form winning race two ahead of Luke Quigley.

BSB Championship Positions

1	BYRNE	95
2	CAMIER	56
3	CRUTCHLOW	55
4	RUTTER	55
5	ELLISON	46
6	M LAVERTY	39

Cup Championship Positions

1	J LAVERTY	85
2	BURNS	56
3	JESSOPP	51
4	ASHLEY	49
5	BUCKINGHAM	42
6	MERCER	41

ROUND

01a

Brands Hatch GP

11th May

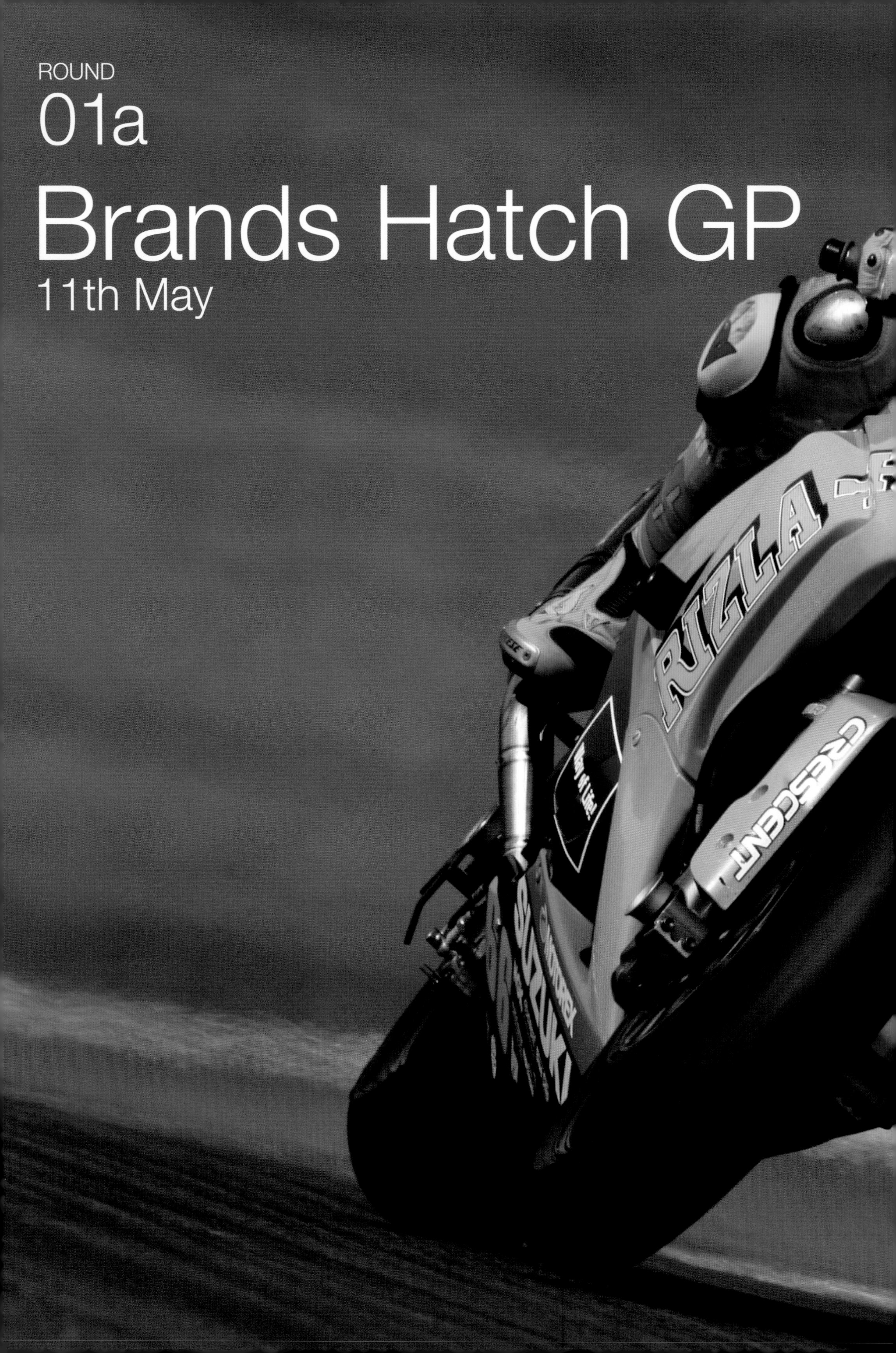

Right: Dave Johnson was trying hard at Brands

Top right: In contrast to the first scheduled date, the sun shone on the massive crowd that witnessed Shane Byrne extend his championship lead at his home circuit

Top: Despite hardly being able to walk and wearing a "Beckham Boot" on his injured foot all weekend, Cal Crutchlow is first into Druids and saw his efforts suitably rewarded with a win in race 2

Brands Hatch GP
11th May

CONTRASTING CONDITIONS AS BYRNE ROLLS ON...

F ive weeks on from the snow aborted opener to the season, hot sun greeted the riders for this rearranged encounter with grid positions as decided back in April, leaving Shane Byrne on pole and poised to take a fourth victory while Cal Crutchlow amazed everyone, including himself, as he won the second race.

That he was on track at all was testament to the skills of the physio at Coventry City FC who had worked intensively to give Crutchlow, who could only just walk with the aid of crutches, a sporting chance but wearing a "Beckham Boot" he was full of fight.

Crutchlow charged into the lead, chased by the hungry Tom Sykes with Byrne in hot pursuit just ahead of Leon Camier and Leon Haslam. Going into the final third of the race, Byrne eased ahead of Sykes to pressurise the leader, Crutchlow, who ran wide at Surtees. Byrne took advantage and with it his third successive win.

Byrne hardly helped his hopes of another double with a sluggish start in race two as Haslam made the running from Crutchlow and Sykes, but he battled back as Haslam had a big moment when the rear of his Honda stepped out of line and dropped him back to eleventh.

Crutchlow led from Sykes and Byrne as the Safety Car intervened following Malcolm Ashley's crash and that bunched the pack, but on the resumption of full racing Sykes was down and out as his Rizla Suzuki bucked wildly out of line in a cloud of smoke. The engine had blown up, and with Byrne and Camier covered in oil, the red flags were quickly out leaving Crutchlow the relieved winner: "If you'd have said a couple of days ago I would have done this, I would have laughed. I was glad the race was stopped as Shane (Byrne) was challenging hard, but I hung on."

That brave ride put Crutchlow into second place in the standings, though still some way down on Byrne, while in the Daily Star Cup there was a first victory of the season for STP MV Agusta rider Chris Burns over Martin Jessopp on the Riders Honda, whereas John Laverty on the Buildbase Ducati took the victory second time out to increase his Championship lead.

BSB Championship Positions			Cup Championship Positions		
1	BYRNE	140	1	J LAVERTY	126
2	CRUTCHLOW	96	2	JESSOPP	87
3	CAMIER	83	3	BURNS	81
4	RUTTER	66	4	QUIGLEY	60
5	ELLISON	64	5	TUNSTALL	52
6	HASLAM	56	6	MORRIS	51

Donington Park

26th May

Top left: Following Ducati's weight penalty, Shakey was put under pressure from the rest of the pack but kept it that way as he pulled off another winning double

Left: Rutter's brakes feel the strain as Luke Quigley's Suzuki breaks under it

Right: James Ellison's MotoGP experience tells as he leads into the Old Hairpin ahead of Haslam, Rutter and Crutchlow

Below: No one has more laps of Donington Park under his belt than Leon Haslam (estimated at over 15,000!), and he was pushing hard all weekend

Donington Park
26th May

BYRNE DEFIES WEIGHT INCREASE TO RECORD DONINGTON DOUBLE...

Controversy reigned in the days leading up to the race as both the Airwaves Ducati and North West 200 Ducati teams reacted angrily to an increase in the minimum weights of their bikes being imposed by the series regulatory body. Both threatened to pull out of the fourth round, but with a compromise put in place on the Friday morning, they raced on.

Byrne made light of those frustrations by taking his third pole start of the season and then transforming that into another winning double while Leon Haslam was enjoying his best day at the races so far this season. He brought his HM Plant Honda home twice in second as Sykes and then Crutchlow claimed the other spots on the podium.

In race one, James Ellison had charged into an early lead but Byrne was soon pegging him back grabbing the lead going through the left/right switch at the Esses. Crutchlow also capitalised on that, taking Ellison, as did Karl Harris, shortly afterwards at Melbourne. Byrne controlled the race from the front, comfortably ahead of Haslam, Sykes, Ellison, Camier, Crutchlow and Karl Harris who was complaining of 'arm-pump.'

In race two, Haslam, who had taken a double at his local circuit in the previous season, took the lead from Ellison just after they had negotiated Redgate Corner for the first time, with Crutchlow soon running second while Byrne, a slow starter, was coming through from sixth.

Byrne's Airwaves Ducati was lapping consistently fast, pegging back time and places and with seven laps remaining he was up to third. Yet again he set the fastest lap of the race and snatched second place from Crutchlow at the Melbourne Hairpin where next time round he confidently took Haslam to win for the sixth time in eight starts.

John Laverty continued his domination of the Daily Star Cup aboard his lightly modified Superstock Ducati, winning the opener from Gary Mason. Mason, who had taken over the Quay Garage Honda ride from the now-retired James Buckingham, had a strong ride in the second race of the day, reversing the result and taking the Cup win from Laverty.

BSB Championship Positions			Cup Championship Positions		
1	BYRNE	190	1	J LAVERTY	171
2	CRUTCHLOW	122	2	JESSOPP	87
3	CAMIER	107	3	TUNSTALL	84
4	HASLAM	96	4	BURNS	81
5	ELLISON	88	5	MORRIS	75
6	RUTTER	82	6	QUIGLEY	73

NO ONE EVER GOT THEIR KNEE DOWN IN A CAR

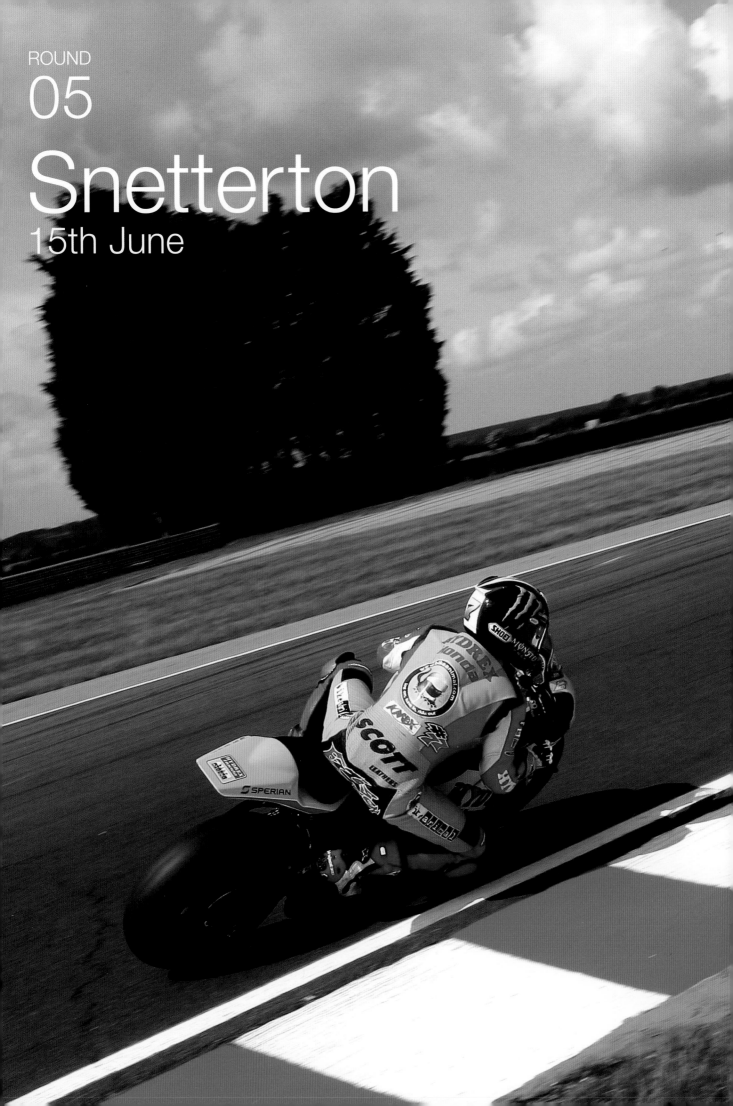

ROUND
05
Snetterton
15th June

Left: Haslam looked left but Rutter squeezed through the narrow gap on the right

Below: Guy Martin was hoping for a change in fortune at Snetterton

Below: Karl Harris and Team boss, Rob McElnea were happy enough on the grid, but Harris jumped off at the Esses causing Shane Byrne to stop to avoid running over him

Above: Leon Camier was in no mood to miss out on his first BSB win and fought with experience beyond his years to hold off Shakey Byrne to take victory in race 1

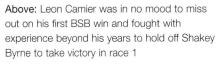

Snetterton
15th June

AIRWAVES DUCATI DOMINATE...

The nature of the Norfolk circuit, with its long Revett Straight, had led many to suggest that this was where the four cylinder bikes would fight back, using their top speed to good effect against the Ducatis, but the hype was hopelessly wrong as the Airwaves-backed bikes in the hands of first Leon Camier and then Shane Byrne took the victories.

Leon Haslam had done his best to break their challenge in the opening race as he made a great start, breaking clear of Camier, Tom Sykes and pole man Byrne but the HM Plant Honda rider was under fire and Camier took him on the third lap. There was little in it and Haslam hit back, regaining the advantage with five laps to go but Camier had the final say at the Esses.

Haslam was then taken by both Byrne and Sykes and with half a mile to go, Byrne snatched the lead from Camier at the Esses, Camier came back, Byrne retaliated at the Bomb Hole before Camier won the dash to the line to take his first ever win in the series.

Delayed by an oil slick from a crashed Supersport bike and then rain, the second race produced a remarkable ride by Byrne. He had to stop on the opening lap to avoid hitting Karl Harris who had highsided right in front of him. He dropped from third to thirteenth but rapidly got his act together and began to carve through the pack.

Camier was leading the action but Byrne was on the charge. "I got going and went for it! I was getting signals that I was picking up places and thought to myself 'keep this pace and you can win'." He was right. Running third at half distance, he was second with a couple of laps to go, making the decisive move on Camier at the Esses to take his seventh victory of the season.

Camier took runner-up spot to maintain his second place in the standings behind runaway leader Byrne while Crutchlow ran third ahead of Rutter and Ellison. Gary Mason powered in a double success in the Daily Star Cup ahead of series leader John Laverty.

BSB Championship Positions

1	BYRNE	235
2	CAMIER	152
3	CRUTCHLOW	151
4	HASLAM	118
5	ELLISON	103
6	RUTTER	102

Cup Championship Positions

1	J LAVERTY	211
2	TUNSTALL	113
3	JESSOPP	109
4	MORRIS	104
5	MASON	95
6	BURNS	81

HENDERSON

INSURANCE BROKERS

Leading independent regional broker with local representation ensuring the highest level of client service

Bespoke solutions for all commercial insurance requirements

Henderson Insurance Brokers Limited has grown to 10 nationwide offices in its 22-year history

More than 200 staff work for the company to provide advice in a clear and precise way

Henderson provide a wide range of specialist divisions that cover every type of business:

Retail • Construction • Haulage •
Professional Indemnity • Healthcare • Corporate •
Surety Services • Risk Management •
Manufacturing

Henderson Insurance Brokers Limited
Trueman House, Capitol Park, Leeds, LS27 0TS
Tel: 0113 393 6300 • Fax: 0113 393 6376

www.hibl.co.uk

Authorised and Regulated by the Financial Services Authority

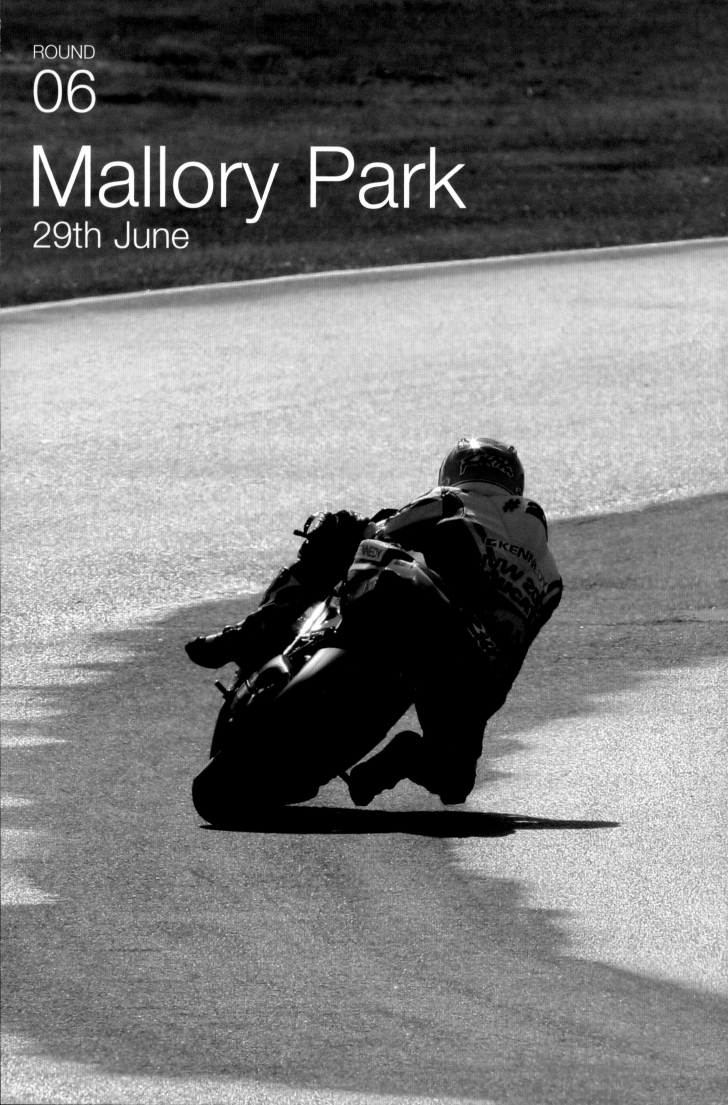

ROUND
06
Mallory Park
29th June

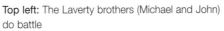

Top left: The Laverty brothers (Michael and John) do battle

Right: Eurosport pundit, James Haydon took over the MSS Kawasaki vacated as a result of Stuart Easton's high speed get off at Snetterton

Left: Crutchlow spins it up through Devils Elbow

Above: Rutter is tight and neat - as he took a tyre gamble, and with it his first BSB win for three years

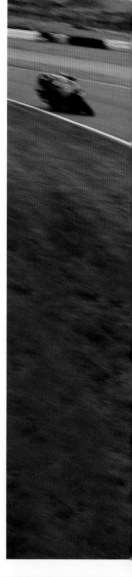

Mallory Park
29th June

RUTTER RULES IN THE RAIN…

Come the halfway stage in the series, Michael Rutter had not tasted the victor's champagne for three long years and that made his victory in the second race all the sweeter. The North West 200 Ducati rider gambled on the weather, opting to run on slicks after rain prior to the start had seen the race declared 'wet.'

Michael Laverty led the pack on his Relentless TAS Suzuki but it was not long before Rutter was out in front. The Ulsterman tipped off, but Rutter was sure-footed as firstly Billy McConnell moved briefly into second before Leon Haslam took over the chase, but Rutter was making good use of the drying lines to pull further clear.

Haslam was struggling with tyre choice and Simon Andrews nosed ahead while Shane Byrne was gathering pace and moved in to attack, going second just before half distance with Cal Crutchlow, Tom Sykes, Karl Harris and Haslam in tow.

Rutter had the victory. "It's a dream, unbelievable," he said while Byrne commented "Michael rode fantastic, the old boy deserved a win." It had been in total contrast to the first race in which Rutter, in his own words, "had a nightmare."

He had to change bikes just before the start, and then had a problem with the traction control system before being thrown over the bars as the Ducati bucked wickedly out of line in the closing stages.

Crutchlow had set the pace ahead of Laverty, Haslam, Byrne and pole-starting Sykes, but as the race began to settle it was Crutchlow leading from his HM Plant Honda teamster Haslam while Laverty and Byrne bashed fairings at the Hairpin. Haslam finally made the telling move on Crutchlow with a dozen laps remaining while Byrne was picking off both Laverty and Sykes to move third.

Byrne took Crutchlow at Gerrards and then accounted for Haslam to win by a second and at the close of the meeting he was some 97 points clear of Crutchlow who had moved second at the expense of first race crasher Leon Camier. John Laverty maintained his lead in the Daily Star Cup with a victory and then a second place to Chris Burns.

BSB Championship Positions

1	BYRNE	280
2	CRUTCHLOW	183
3	CAMIER	160
4	HASLAM	148
5	RUTTER	127
6	SYKES	126

Cup Championship Positions

1	J LAVERTY	256
2	TUNSTALL	140
3	JESSOPP	135
4	MASON	126
5	BURNS	122
6	MORRIS	104

MOTORCYCLE FINANCE

Unleash the Horsepower

Team Black Horse

Be part of the team

With our finance deals, the biggest problem you'll have is which bike to choose.

Go to your chosen dealer for more details.

Oulton Park
20th July

Above: Ellison obviously enjoyed Oulton first time around and came back for more

Below: MSS Kawasaki boss Nick Morgan finds out how tough things are on the other side of the camera

Crutchlow pushes hard, as does Sykes while Haslam leads the pack into Lodge

Some keep it up – others put it down - Oulton Park is all about wheels up, getting crossed up, or spinning up!

Oulton Park
20th July

SYKES AT THE DOUBLE...

Tom Sykes took a stunning debut winning double to give the Rizla Suzuki team their best result in four long years since John Reynolds had achieved two victories in an afternoon, also at the Cheshire circuit.

"This is something else, something special" enthused Sykes, as he savoured his first successes in the top flight. "It's a bit like waiting for the Number 10 bus to come along, you have a long wait and then two come together!" before adding with a smile "I'll be making a brew and having a slice of cake to celebrate, and then maybe some fast food on the way home!"

Sykes had led initially from James Ellison, Leon Haslam, Karl Harris and pole starter Cal Crutchlow, but soon it was the Hydrex Bike Animal Honda in the hands of Ellison running out front, however, the Suzuki rider regained the lead at Hizzy's.

Shane Byrne, the lone Airwaves Ducati rider after Leon Camier's heavy crash in qualifying had ruled him out, was making up ground when he tangled with Harris who had run a bit wide at the Shell Oils hairpin. Byrne went for the inside but as the Yamaha closed back, they touched. Harris was down and out, Byrne managed to continue.

Race officials studied the incident, but took no action, as meanwhile Crutchlow erred, running wide and losing five places before fighting back. But Sykes was ruling supreme taking his first victory by almost five seconds from Ellison, Byrne and Haslam.

It was Haslam who roared away at the start of the second race but he was soon pegged back by the confident Sykes who was ahead on the second lap and settling into a rhythm that made him unbeatable. Crutchlow held on to second, though not without a last lap shoot-out with Byrne who had briefly nosed ahead but could not make the move stick. Haslam was fourth ahead of Ellison.

Byrne, with a pair of third places, increased his lead in the standings to 99 points over Crutchlow with Sykes moving third at the expense of Haslam, while in the Daily Star Cup John Laverty was continuing his unrelenting ride to the title with a second winning double of the campaign ahead of first Martin Jessopp and then Chris Burns.

BSB Championship Positions

1	BYRNE	312
2	CRUTCHLOW	213
3	SYKES	176
4	HASLAM	174
5	CAMIER	160
6	ELLISON	150

Cup Championship Positions

1	J LAVERTY	306
2	JESSOPP	171
3	TUNSTALL	166
4	MASON	146
5	BURNS	122
6	MORRIS	104

The Sound of Performance

The legendary YZF-R1 evolves. Yamaha's new superbike represents the most significant development in engine and chassis technology ever seen in the 11-year history of this legendary motorcycle. The all-new 998cc engine has been influenced by the powerplant of our championship winning YZF-M1 in design, feel and character.

In addition, the completely redesigned aluminium Deltabox chassis and aggressive new styling give the new-generation YZF-R1 a radical new look too.

Get yourself down to you local autthorised Yamaha dealer or click on our website for more information on this and the entire range of 2009 Yamaha motorcycles and accessories. Be prepared to see and hear the future.

YAMALUBE

2008
Valentino Rossi
World Champion
MotoGP
YAMAHA

2008
Manufacturers
World Champion
MotoGP
YAMAHA

2008
Team
World Champion
MotoGP
YAMAHA

www.yamaha-motor.co.uk

Knockhill

10th August

Top left: Once again, Rutter excelled in the drying conditions

Above: Scott Smart's Hawk Kawasaki was spitting fire at those behind

Opposite: Shane Byrne shows Guy Martin the fast line round Knockhill - as Martin would undoubtedly show Byrne down Bray Hill?

Above: Rutter and Sykes came to blows resulting in Rutter's damaged quickshift

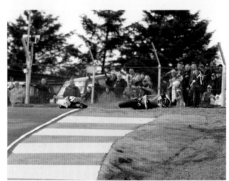  

Sequence: Shakey Byrne flies high as he crashes out of race two

Left: Cal Crutchlow wore one of his friend Craig Jones' helmets as a tribute to the former British star who had tragically lost his life in a racing accident earlier in the month

Knockhill
10th August

CRUTCHLOW, BYRNE AND HASLAM CRASH OUT IN SCOTLAND...

Tom Sykes won the opening race in the damp, continuing his rich vein of form but there was no action replay for the Rizla Suzuki rider in a dramatic second race.

It was red-flagged because of rain on the sighting lap, stopped at one-third distance by a three rider tangle, and then halted five laps early when the series leader Shane Byrne took his second tumble of the weekend.

Leon Haslam broke his seasonal duck, ending a run of 17 races without a win and there was some cheer for Karl Harris who finally ended his run of ill-fortune, though for others, that was not the case. Stuart Easton's return from a broken wrist was abortive and then John Laverty was ruled out after a heavy crash in opening free practice.

Haslam chalked up his first pole start of the season but in the opening race, declared wet, it was Michael Rutter who led on the drying lines from Sykes and Haslam with James Ellison ahead of Byrne while Cal Crutchlow tipped off early on.

On the ninth lap Sykes finally found a way past Rutter, who was wrestling with a broken quick-shift, seconds before Haslam, himself struggling with a technical problem, slid out. Byrne was moving through, going second at two-thirds distance, but Sykes had the telling edge.

In race two, Haslam was keen to make amends for his earlier demise, scorching into the lead ahead of first Rutter and then Byrne before the race was stopped as three riders went down. At the re-start, Byrne was soon out front though Haslam was full of fight and making inroads into his lead when Byrne crashed heavily at the first turn on the fifteenth lap.

It was the first non-finish of the year for Shakey and he was lucky to escape with just a bruising while Haslam had the victory, ahead of Rutter and Harris, and in the Daily Star Cup there were victories for Gary Mason and Chris Burns.

It had been an eventful day, and one tinged with sadness, as the whole of the BSB community remembered one of their own, Craig Jones who had been fatally injured in a World Supersport race earlier in the month.

BSB Championship Positions		
1	BYRNE	332
2	CRUTCHLOW	222
3	SYKES	214
4	HASLAM	199
5	CAMIER	179
6	ELLISON	177

Cup Championship Positions		
1	J LAVERTY	306
2	JESSOPP	211
3	TUNSTALL	188
4	MASON	187
5	BURNS	163
6	MORRIS	117

OPEN IT UP

SWAN COMBI - A WINNING TEAM
50 FILTERS AND 50 PAPERS TOGETHER IN ONE POCKET HANDY PACK

Cadwell Park

5th August

Above: Shakey works the Airwaves Ducati - Same line, same style - every time!

Top right: Haslam may have taken the two wins, but there were battles raging right through the field

Top left: Once again, Karl 'Bomber' Harris was King of the Mountain

Right: Leon Camier rounds Barn Corner under the beautiful Cadwell Park trees

Left: There is only one dry line – and it is not very wide!

Bottom: Crutchlow on the limit through Hall Bends

Cadwell Park
25th August

HASLAM DOUBLES UP…

Leon Haslam had a record to protect in these races as he had won a Superbike race in each of his previous visits to Cadwell, the home circuit of his HM Plant Honda team, and he was intent on doing the business for them. He did just that, taking a deserved winning double.

Ahead of the races, there had been the newly introduced F1 style shoot-out for pole with a three-stage process ensuring that everyone had to be out, and on the pace in the opening part to ensure a place in the twenty riders going forward to the second part. In turn, this halved the number going into the final dash for pole that was won by Tom Sykes as the new format won wide acclaim from riders, teams and fans alike.

Sykes had his Rizla Suzuki at the head of the pack with Haslam not far down as Cal Crutchlow, Michael Rutter and Shane Byrne ran in hot pursuit while Karl Harris and Dave Johnson were early casualties. Haslam was closing in on the leader Sykes before making his decisive move on the eleventh lap at Park to take the victory by half a second with Byrne third from Camier, Crutchlow, Rutter and Simon Andrews. Gary Mason won the Daily Star Cup category but any hopes of a double ended abruptly on the opening lap of the second race when he crashed spectacularly.

In that second race, Sykes ran clear early on from Crutchlow, who clipped the kerb at Hall Bends and went down before wrestling the bike back upright to score an eventual couple of points. Haslam, riding superbly, upped the pressure on Sykes, taking the lead on the seventh lap, and then holding his advantage to complete a hat-trick of Cadwell victories which moved him into third place in the overall standings, just five points down on Sykes. Byrne completed the podium finishers to leave the circuit a massive 110 points clear in the title stakes.

John Laverty, second to Mason in the opening race, headed off Chris Burns to take his eighth Daily Star Cup success and move closer to the title with a huge 111 points lead over Martin Jessopp, who claimed a fourth and third place.

BSB Championship Positions

1	BYRNE	364
2	SYKES	254
3	HASLAM	249
4	CRUTCHLOW	236
5	CAMIER	205
6	RUTTER	195

Cup Championship Positions

1	J LAVERTY	351
2	JESSOPP	240
3	MASON	212
4	TUNSTALL	211
5	BURNS	199
6	MORRIS	135

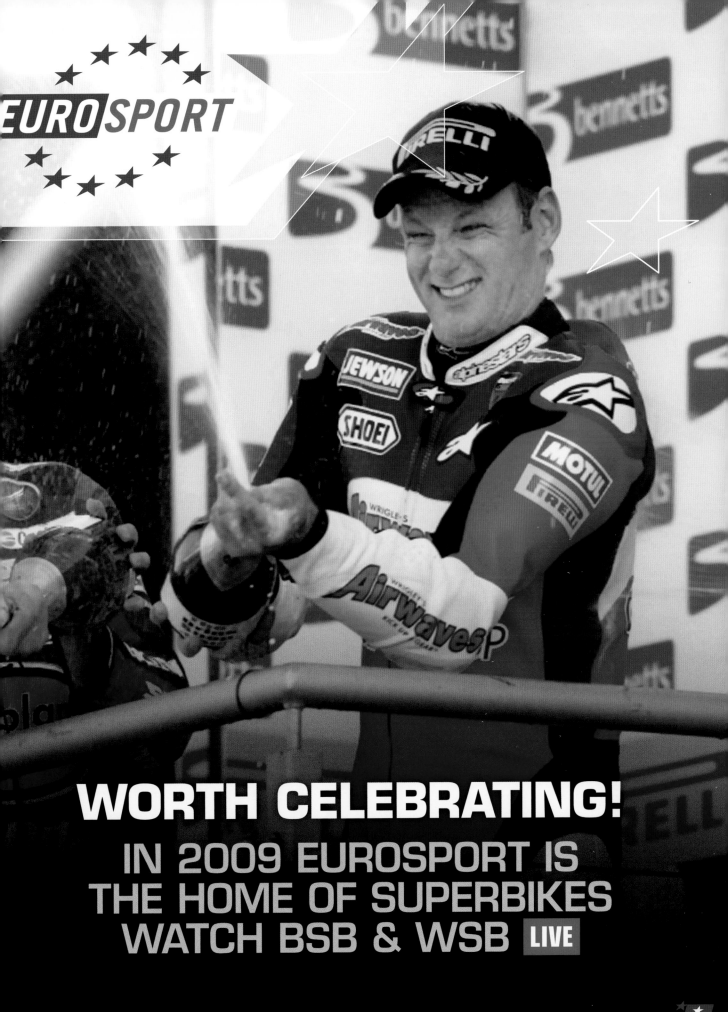

WORTH CELEBRATING!

IN 2009 EUROSPORT IS
THE HOME OF SUPERBIKES
WATCH BSB & WSB LIVE

ROUND

10

Croft

14th September

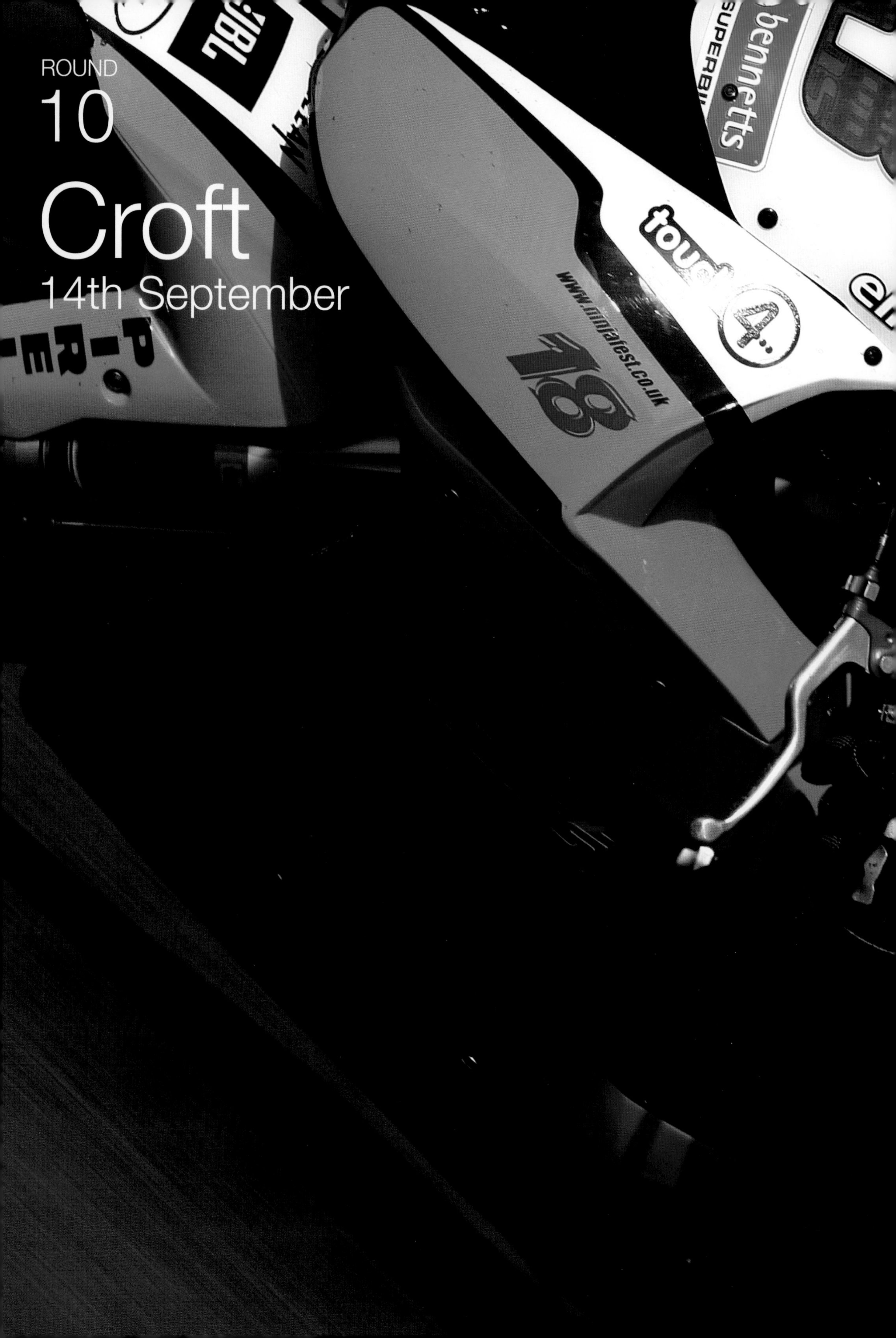

Tight to the end - close battles were the order of the day

Top right: Some were closer than others!

Far right: Camier shows a clean pair of heels

Below right: Camier celebrates his race one win

Bottom left: As new boy, Jason O'Halloran plants himself firmly on the tarmac

Right: 'Grinner' hoists a high one

Top right: Crutchlow takes the hole-shot from Rutter, Sykes and Haslam

Bottom right: The HM Plant Honda 'syncro pair' in close action

Croft
14th September

KINGS OF LEON AS LAVERTY CLAIMS CUP...

Leon Camier and Leon Haslam took the victories on an afternoon of frustration for Shane Byrne, who had lost a couple of teeth in a heavy crash during free practice, and after missing out on a pair of podium finishes, he saw the chance of sealing the title for a second time in five years at the North Yorkshire circuit slip from his grasp.

There had been incident and controversy in the opening race when Byrne had gone into the hairpin for the last time running in third only to be barged back to fifth as Tom Sykes went for the inside line and took the sixteen points.

Rizla Suzuki rider Sykes had led from the start of that race from Crutchlow, Haslam and Byrne while Michael Rutter was just ahead of Leon Camier. Haslam took over out front at Tower on the eighth lap while Camier was on the ascendancy and soon running second with Sykes protecting third from Byrne. Meanwhile Crutchlow was suffering with a gear problem and lost a little ground. Camier decisively took the lead at Tower with eight laps to go and held on to the flag.

Race two saw pole sitter Crutchlow take charge with Sykes, Rutter, Camier and Haslam in the mix. Byrne was playing catch up in tenth place after a dreadful start. Sykes, whose move to World Superbikes with Yamaha had been confirmed over the weekend, was keen to show why and he grabbed the lead at half distance only to be thwarted by Haslam's speed on the penultimate lap which ensured his victory.

Byrne was up to fourth but Crutchlow just held him off as the champion elect fell six points short of the title. "It's been a bad day at the office and I'm gutted that I didn't get on the podium in either race. In the first race I worked hard to get third but was pushed very wide at the final corner and driven back to fifth. It has been frustrating," said Byrne.

There was title cheer for John Laverty, despite continuing pain from his knee injuries as a pair of seconds gave him the Daily Star Cup even though Gary Mason won both races.

BSB Championship Positions

1	BYRNE	388
2	HASLAM	294
3	SYKES	290
4	CRUTCHLOW	265
5	CAMIER	241
6	RUTTER	215

Cup Championship Positions

1	J LAVERTY	391
2	JESSOPP	264
3	MASON	262
4	TUNSTALL	238
5	BURNS	215
6	MORRIS	135

italian modern art

by Sidi.

...say hello to the New Vortice

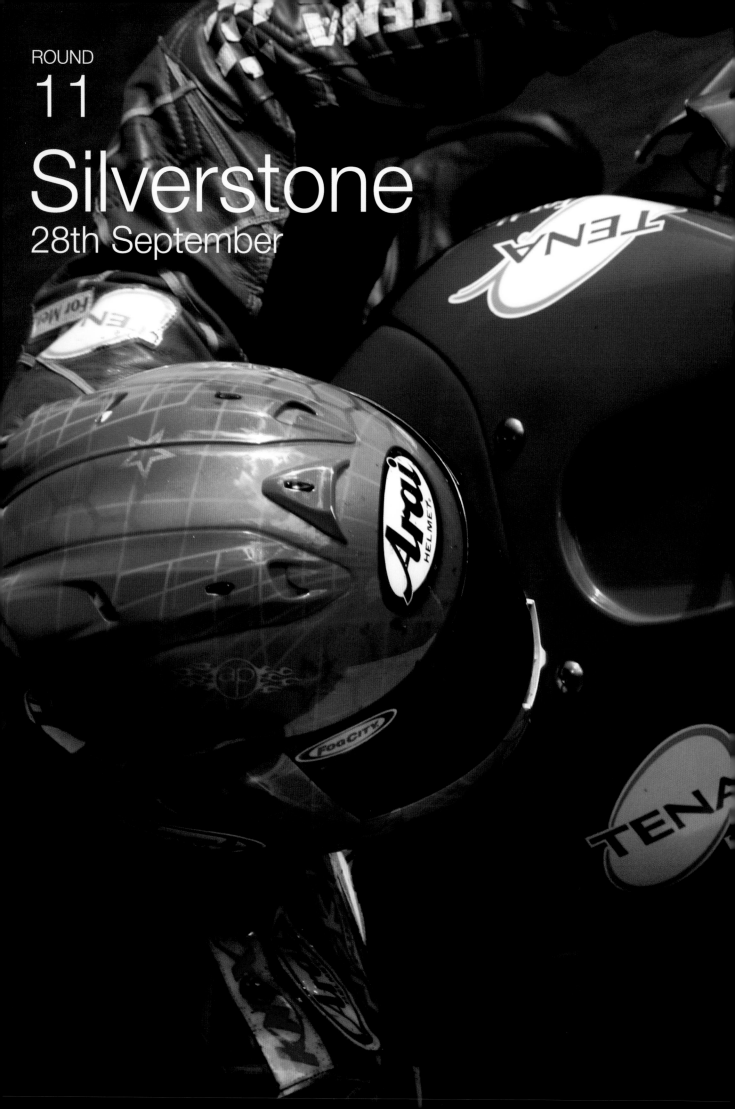

ROUND
11
Silverstone
28th September

Top left: Crutchlow blasts out of the shadows

Far left: Not such a Shakey start as Byrne gets a flyer

Left: Ouch . . . You can almost hear the suspension crying 'enough!' as Camier gets some serious power down

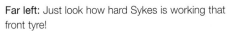

Far left: Just look how hard Sykes is working that front tyre!

Left: Cal Crutchlow is oblivious as Michael Laverty is left to pick up the pieces after having his Relentless Suzuki taken out by an out of control James Ellison

Below left: Harris keeps it neat at Bridge

Sequence: Any slight Championship hopes held by Haslam and Sykes were dashed as 'The Grinner' took out Haslam at the chicane with a rash move for which he was later penalised

Far left: Rutter continued to push hard

Left: Shakey crosses the line to take the Title

Silverstone
28th September

SHAKEY SEALS THE DEAL...

Shane Byrne sealed the crown with a solid ride into third place in the opening race of the penultimate round which was won by his Airwaves Ducati team-mate Leon Camier, ahead of Cal Crutchlow.

"Words can't describe what this all means to me; it is bigger for me than the first time that I won the title. This repays the team for their faith in me and this has paid everything back and thanks to my sponsors," said Byrne who added: "This is dedicated to my dad Pete who died a month before the season started. I hope that he is up there smiling down on me, he backed me so much."

Byrne had gone into the race needing a top nine finish to take the title, and he was running eighth when everything happened in front of him. Leon Haslam, the leader, was sent crashing by Tom Sykes, who was later penalised for his clattering move at the chicane, then Karl Harris went grass-tracking, while James Ellison highsided going into the chicane, taking out Michael Laverty.

Byrne was running third, more than enough, as he settled for strong points to regain the title he had first won in 2003. Haslam who had wrestled his bike back on track to take twelfth place in that first race heeded the advice of his HM Plant Honda team that the best way to keep out of trouble was to charge clear of the pack in race two.

He did that to good effect, taking his fifth victory in seven races, by some four seconds from Byrne who was not able to make any impression on the leader. Sykes took third place, despite being demoted a dozen places on the grid, to the fifth row, for his earlier indiscretion. Camier, Harris and James Ellison trailed them in.

Gary Mason was the first of the Daily Star Cup finishers on the road in each race, but at Technical Control when his Quay Garage Honda was examined a camshaft irregularity was discovered leading to his exclusion. Chris Burns and the champion John Laverty were credited with the victories.

BSB Championship Positions

1	BYRNE	424
2	HASLAM	324
3	SYKES	306
4	CRUTCHLOW	285
5	CAMIER	279
6	RUTTER	237

Cup Championship Positions

1	J LAVERTY	424
2	JESSOPP	304
3	TUNSTALL	264
4	MASON	262
5	BURNS	240
6	MORRIS	156

PREMIUM HELMETS

WORN BY CHAMPIONS

Sequence: Leon Haslam takes yet another beating as he high-sides from his HM Plant Honda

Left: Wearing his magnificent Championship winners helmet - (specially prepared by Shoei), Byrne and Haslam had an epic battle in the final race of the season - Byrne eventually coming out on top and signing off the season in the style of a true Champion

Bottom right: Stuart Easton got caught out on the white line at the bottom of Paddock Hill but, unlike many others, managed to stay on board!

Top left: Haslam heads the pack in the late summer sun

Left: Michael Rutter started his landmark 300th BSB race

Left: Camier and Sykes both pushed hard as they fought for their final Championship points of the season

Above: Shakey celebrates with the man who made it all possible - GSE's Darrell Healey

Brands Hatch Indy
12th October

BYRNE BOWS OUT IN STYLE...

Shane Byrne bid farewell to the domestic series in true champion's style as he not only claimed his fifth pole position of the season, but signed off with a fantastic race winning double.

The Airwaves Ducati rider had sealed the championship for the second time in five years at the penultimate round at Silverstone meaning the pressure was off and in the opening race, once he had taken Cal Crutchlow at Druids on the second lap, he romped home unchallenged for the victory.

James Ellison battled hard with the injured Leon Haslam who was riding with a damaged shoulder, the legacy of a qualifying crash, for the final podium placing as a capacity crowd looked on in glorious end of season sunshine. The second race however was a different story with Haslam, despite his painful injuries, making the running and leaving Byrne playing catch up, but the champion was equal to the challenge.

Moving through from fourth, he was second at half distance but then turned on the speed and style to reel in the leading HM Plant Honda, snatching the lead on the final lap as they carved through back markers in one of the classic BSB races of all time.

Haslam took some consolation with his second place, as coupled with the earlier fourth position, it gave him the overall runner-up place in the rankings. Crutchlow, who mirrored his team-mate's results, was third overall in the standings from Tom Sykes whose season ended on a disappointing note with a sixth place in race one but retired from race two with machine problems.

Mason, whose bike was later stripped and found to be entirely legal, took the Daily Star Cup honours in race one, ahead of champion John Laverty, with the roles being reversed after a titanic battle between the pair in race two which also went down to the wire.

So, as the sun set on the 2008 season, amidst a myriad of tyre smoke and burning rubber, the riders launched their kit and caboodle into the crowd before acclaiming Shakey on the winners' podium. Then, once the smoke had settled, out came double World Superbike Champion James Toseland to play an impromptu gig on the keyboard as he acclaimed Byrne as the worthy winner.

It could only happen in BSB...

BSB Final Championship Positions			Cup Final Championship Positions		
1	BYRNE	474	1	J LAVERTY	469
2	HASLAM	357	2	JESSOPP	328
3	CRUTCHLOW	318	3	MASON	307
4	SYKES	316	4	TUNSTALL	283
5	CAMIER	306	5	BURNS	267
6	RUTTER	256	6	MORRIS	165

Daily Star Superbike Cup

LAVERTY - THE CHAMPION WHO SHOULD NEVER HAVE BEEN...

John Laverty ended up winning the Daily Star Cup for BSB Privateers when he really shouldn't have been racing in the series!

The 26-year-old Ulsterman had originally planned to campaign his 1098cc Buildbase Ducati in the National Superstock 1000 Championship but when a last minute problem with not enough of the exotic Italian twins being homologated was identified, the JHR team, which runs Michael Rutter in NW200 colours, decided to go and source the extra budget needed in order to run 'J Lav' in the premier class which was achieved with only days to spare.

The middle of the three racing brothers from Toomebridge in County Antrim, repaid the team and the organisers, who had temporarily waived certain rules to accommodate the bike, with a string of great results starting with a double at the opening Thruxton round before taking race wins at Oulton, Brands and Donington to stamp his authority on proceedings.

Mallory was one of only three meetings all season long where he didn't claim at least one winner's trophy, the others being at Knockhill where he ruled himself out of the meeting with a big crash on Friday and at Croft where he became the first rider in all of the regular BSB classes to wrap up a title.

Another rider who was also not in the pre-season plans ended up third in the shape of former works rider Gary Mason. Without a ride after a difficult year in America, the 29-year-old was drafted into the Quay Garage Honda team when former Superbike Cup Champion James Buckingham quit at Brands Hatch in round three. The ex Virgin Yamaha and Stobart Honda rider more or less matched Laverty from round four onwards and had his double victory at Silverstone been allowed to stand, he'd have secured runner-up spot in the series. As it turned out, a post-race check found an illegal component in the engine and he was stripped of the fifty points that day.

Taking runner up spot as a result was the consistent Martin Jessopp on the Riders Honda who, despite finishing in every race bar two, never claimed the top step of the podium, instead boxing off ten podiums along the way and more importantly for him, netting the £4000 prize as the Airwaves Kick Up A Gear winner.

Chris Burns showed glimpses of his brilliance and the MV's potential with four wins along the way, interspersed with a number of mechanical breakdowns as he and Yamaha rookie Steve Mercer were the only other riders to claim wins.

Championship Positions

1	John LAVERTY	469
2	Martin JESSOPP	328
3	Gary MASON	307
4	Tom TUNSTALL	283
5	Chris BURNS	267
6	Leon MORRIS	165

Fuchs-Silkolene
British Supersport
Championship

KING RICHARDS…

Aussie Glen Richards proved to be the class of the field by winning the title with a round to spare and then ramming home the fact in emphatic fashion by taking a win at the final round.

The MAP Embassy Triumph rider won only once in the opening six races, courtesy of an outrageous pass on arch-rival Hudson Kennaugh on the final corner at Oulton Park in May but thereafter, had to wait until the second Oulton visit before sampling the winner's champagne again.

Victory at Croft over the South African Kennaugh, put him in the driving seat and his fourth position at Silverstone was enough to take the title on the same weekend as his team announced their withdrawal from the sport.

Kennaugh took the win at Silverstone to add to the Raceways Yamaha team's victories at Brands GP and in the wet at Mallory, whereas HM Plant Honda's Steve Brogan had drawn first blood at Thruxton only for his bid to fizzle out in mid-season as he concentrated on winning the Superstock 1000 crown.

Fresh from his debut TT victory, Steve Plater (AIM Yamaha) won at Snetterton and again at his local Cadwell Park whilst another double victory went the way of Relentless Suzuki rider Ian Lowry at Knockhill to add to the win he inherited at Donington when Hannspree Ten Kate riders Andrew Pitt and Jonathan Rea were subsequently excluded.

In the Supersport Cup, Craig Fitzpatrick also wrapped up the title at Silverstone ahead of Andy Weymouth, ending the season with a total of eight victories.

Championship Positions

1	Glen RICHARDS (Triumph)	240
2	Hudson KENNAUGH (Yamaha)	187
3	Ian LOWRY (Suzuki)	146
4	James WESTMORELAND (Honda)	136
5	Steve PLATER (Yamaha)	106
6	Chris MARTIN (Kawasaki)	99

Metzeler National
Superstock 1000
Championship

BROGAN EVENTUALLY DOES IT…

Winning eight of the twelve rounds should have made winning the title easy for Liverpudlian Steve Brogan but the fact that it took the factory-supported Honda UK rider until the penultimate round at Silverstone to box off the title showed just how hard it was.

Compounding the situation was the fact that in the other four races, he finished runner-up in three of them with a worst result of the season coming at Croft with fourth, which speaks volumes about Jon Kirkham (Raceways Yamaha) who chased him relentlessly throughout the season.

Kirkham beat Brogan on three occasions, the only one time that either one of them didn't top the podium was at Donington Park when Marshall Neill sneaked in for the win at a time when Kirkham was back in the truck after his race ended with a holed radiator on the warm up lap.

Other than that, it really was a two horse race for the crown although it was anything less in the battle for third place overall, which was eventually claimed by Peter Hickman who emerged from Brands as one of six riders covered by eighteen points who could have claimed it!

Alastair Seeley took fourth ahead of Ben Wilson with sixth placed Adrian Coates announcing his retirement at the end of the season.

Championship Positions

1	Steve BROGAN *(Honda)*	273
2	Jon KIRKHAM *(Yamaha)*	215
3	Peter HICKMAN *(Yamaha)*	125
4	Alistair SEELEY *(Yamaha)*	108
5	Ben WILSON *(Yamaha)*	103
6	Adrian COATES *(Yamaha)*	102

Metzeler National
Superstock 600
Championship

POINTS MAKE PRIZES FOR JOHNSTON…

The inaugural Superstock 600 class will be remembered for both the packed grids and the close racing as the Stars of Tomorrow battled it out for supremacy.

With such illustrious names as Tommy Hill, Tom Sykes and Craig Jones emanating from the previous incarnation 'Junior Superstock' back at the turn of the decade, now it was Ulsterman Lee Johnston who added his name to the Hall of Fame after proving that points really do make prizes.

'The General' took victory in only one race all season long, that coming his way at Knockhill, but the fact that he was prepared to rack up the points and the podiums along the way, whilst many of his rivals were falling down, saw him clinch the title with a round to spare.

Giving chase throughout was Robbie Brown who took four wins along the way but significantly, failure to score at both Oulton Park and Silverstone, where he crashed out, meant the best he could do was runner-up spot.

2007 125cc British Champion Luke Jones was another rider that could have made a serious bid for the title as he won three out of the opening five races but a testing crash at Knockhill ruled him out for a couple of rounds although he did bounce back to win at Silverstone.

Other winners included South African Allan Jon Venter as well as a certain Jimmy Hill, the younger brother of WSB star Tommy, and had it not been for a crash in the final round at Brands, it could have been a hat-trick for him.

Championship Positions

1	Lee JOHNSTON *(Yamaha)*	207
2	Robbie BROWN *(Yamaha)*	166
3	Chris NORTHOVER *(Yamaha)*	135
4	AJ VENTER *(Triumph)*	132
5	Luke JONES *(Yamaha)*	124
6	Jimmy HILL *(Yamaha)*	112

Relentless British 125GP Championship

PEANUT POWERS THROUGH...

The closest out of all the championships went right down to the wire at the final round at a sun-kissed Brands Hatch with Matthew 'Peanut' Hoyle holding a slender eight point advantage over Timmy 'The Twister' Hastings.

Having won 50% of the races, Hoyle should have boxed off the title in plenty of time but due to his commitments in the Red Bull Rookies MotoGP Cup, it meant he missed out at Croft when racing at Indianapolis and although making the overnight dash back from Assen to Mallory, his four points from that double-header weekend saw the series kept alive until the bitter end.

Taking maximum advantage of Hoyle's absence at Croft, Hastings won up in Yorkshire and the pair arrived at Brands to slug it out. The title swung back and forth as the leaders diced but on lap six, down went Hastings in a cloud of dust at Paddock Hill Bend meaning Hoyle was champion irrespective of the race result.

It was a sad end to the season for the wee Scot, who for consolation took the ACU Academy Cup ahead of Hoyle as other race winners included Paul Jordan, Lee Costello, Martin Glossop and James Lodge.

Emerging talent in the shape of Taylor Mackenzie and Corey Lewis meant they are riders to watch in 2009 and beyond as veteran ambassador for the 125cc class, Michael Wilcox, announced his retirement following a big accident at Knockhill.

Championship Positions

1	Matthew HOYLE *(Honda)*	190
2	Timmy HASTINGS *(Honda)*	162
3	Paul JORDAN *(Honda)*	135
4	Tom HAYWARD *(Honda)*	134
5	Connor BEHAN *(Honda)*	118
6	James LODGE *(Honda)*	109

KIRKHAM AT A CANTER…

It wasn't just a case of winning the title, it was more like world domination as Jon Kirkham tied up just about everything going in the series that replaced the Virgin Media Cup after a five-year stint.

The field oozed quality if not quantity but quite simply, from the point that the tall Derbyshire rider took the chequered flag at Thruxton in April to the time he did likewise at Brands in October, he was simply a cut above the rest.

Just three times was he beaten all season long and that included the double-header, non-championship support race at the British GP as well as the interspersed Spring and Autumn Cup for good measure.

Sam Warren took the win in the damp at Oulton Park as he exercised his Supermoto skills in the tricky conditions and then after JK had crashed out and remounted at both Snetterton and Knockhill, it was left to Richard Cooper and Ben Wilson to win each of those respective races.

Warren claimed runner-up place in the Spring Cup with Wilson doing likewise in both the Autumn Cup and main championship after an early season challenge from veteran Sean Emmett came to a halt when he quit the series mid-season and the impressive Gary Mason did likewise towards the end of the year to concentrate on his British Superbike commitments with the Quay Garage Honda team.

Championship Positions

1	Jon KIRKHAM	250
2	Ben WILSON	212
3	Sam WARREN	147
4	Adrian COATES	130
5	Gary MASON	121
6	Jack KENNEDY	86

Focused
Events KTM
Super Duke Battle

WOODY PECKS 'EM...

Former British Superbike Championship rider David Wood turned in a 'super-human' performance to win the second annual series for the naked street fighters.

Often resplendent in his cartoon-character leathers of either 'Woody' (from Toy Story) or Superman, ever the comedian, Wood won eight races on the way to the title after seeing off an early season challenge from Kelvin Reilly.

Reilly took his one and only victory of the series in the wet at Donington to clinch runner-up spot in the title chase but had it not been for previous commitments in the USA and in the Endurance World Championship, then triple winner Richard Cooper could well have mounted a serious title challenge.

Bike racing journalists Alistair Fagan, Jonathan Pearson and Bruce Wilson were all in the mix throughout the season at various points on the 'guest bike' meaning plenty of column inches for the series in the various mags!

Championship Positions

1	David WOOD	256
2	Kelvin REILLY	205
3	Ed SMITH	142
4	Dave HEAL	142
5	Richard COOPER	135
6	James EDMEADES	134

Behind the scenes

CIRCUIT CLOSED
STRICTLY NO ADMITTANCE

2008 Bennetts British Superbike Championship

Points after final round

Round/venue key (each round comprises two races):
- Round 02 – Thruxton, 20 April 2008 → R3, R4
- Round 03 – Oulton Park, 5 May 2008 → R5, R6
- Round 1a – Brands Hatch GP, 11 May 2008 → R1, R2
- Round 04 – Donington Park, 26 May 2008 → R7, R8
- Round 05 – Snetterton, 15 June 2008 → R9, R10
- Round 06 – Mallory Park, 29 June 2008 → R11, R12
- Round 07 – Oulton Park, 20 July 2008 → R13, R14
- Round 08 – Knockhill, 10 August 2008 → R15, R16
- Round 09 – Cadwell Park, 25 August 2008 → R17, R18
- Round 10 – Croft, 14 September 2008 → R19, R20
- Round 11 – Silverstone, 28 September 2008 → R21, R22
- Round 12 – Brands Hatch Indy, 12 October 2008 → R23, R24

Name	Total	R3	R4	R5	R6	R1	R2	R7	R8	R9	R10	R11	R12	R13	R14	R15	R16	R17	R18	R19	R20	R21	R22	R23	R24
Shayne BYRNE (Ducati)	474	25	20	25	25	25	20	25	25	20	25	25	20	16	16	20		16	16	11	13	16	20	25	25
Leon HASLAM (Honda)	357	13		20		13	10	20	20	11	11	20	10	13	13		25	25	25	20	25	5	25	13	20
Cal CRUTCHLOW (Honda)	318	20	25	10		16	25	10	16	13	16	16	16	10	20		9	11	3	13	16	20		20	13
Tom SYKES (Suzuki)	316	10	8	11		20		16	10	16	9	13	13	25	25	25	13	20	20	16	20		16	10	
Leon CAMIER (Ducati)	306	11	13	16	16	11	16	11	13	25	20		8			11	8	13	13	25	11	25	13	11	16
Michael RUTTER (Ducati)	256	16	16	13	10		11	8	8	7	13		25	9	5	13	20	10	11	10	10	13	9	9	10
James ELLISON (Honda)	230	9	9	8	20	10	8	13	11	9	6	11	5	20	11	16	11			7	9		10	16	11
Simon ANDREWS (Yamaha)	176	8			9	7		6	7	6	8	9	9	11	10	8	10	9	10	6	7	11	8	8	9
Michael LAVERTY (Suzuki)	141	6	11	9	13				13	7		10	10	5		7	9	10		8	7	9	6		1
Tristan PALMER (Honda)	111	3	3	7	5	6	5	4	2	3	7	8	7		4	7	4	5	4	2	2	10	4	6	3
Karl HARRIS (Yamaha)	102									9	9	8			11	7		9	16		6	8	8	11	
Billy McCONNELL (Kawasaki)	91	2	6		6	8	7	5	5	10				8	6			7		4		6	7	4	
Stuart EASTON (Kawasaki)	81	7	10	6	11	9	9	5	5										2	1	3	8	5		
Atsushi WATANABE (Suzuki)	69		2	3	7	4			3	4		7			3		1	7	9	4	4	7		2	2
Scott SMART (Kawasaki)	69		4	5	8			5	6	1	4		6	5	8		3	3	8	3					
Gary MASON (Honda)	51										6			2	4	3	3	6	6		6	2	1	5	7
John LAVERTY (Ducati)	49	4	5		3				3			6	2	6	3			2	1				3	3	8
Guy MARTIN (Honda)	28	1	7	4		3	4										2	1	5						1
Jason O'HALLORAN (Honda)	21																				1	9	6	1	4
Chris BURNS (MV Agusta)	21					2						1	3			1	6					3			5
David JOHNSON (Honda)	21			2							2	4	4			3						4	2		
Jon KIRKHAM (Yamaha)	13																							7	6
Steve MERCER (Yamaha)	10			1												4	5								
Tom GRANT (Honda)	10				1			3						1		5									
Dean ELLISON (Yamaha)	9	1	1							2	1			2	2										
James HAYDON (Kawasaki)	6												1	4	1										
Sean EMMETT (Yamaha)	5	5																							
Steve PLATER (Yamaha)	4				4																				
Marshall NEILL (Honda)	4									1	3														
Martin JESSOPP (Honda)	4					1								2								1			
Luke QUIGLEY (Suzuki)	3				2	1																			
Aaron ZANOTTI (Honda)	2					2																			
Peter HICKMAN (Honda)	2																					2			

2008 British Superbike Daily Star Cup

Points after final round

Name	Total	R3	R4	R5	R6	R1	R2	R7	R8	R9	R10	R11	R12	R13	R14	R15	R16	R17	R18	R19	R20	R21	R22	R23	R24
John LAVERTY (Ducati)	469	25	25	10	25	16	25	25	20	20	20	25	20	25	25	20	25	25	25			8	25	20	25
Martin JESSOPP (Honda)	328	10	20	8	13	20	16					11	11	13	13	20	16	13	16	13	11	20	20	13	11
Gary MASON (Honda)	307							20	25	25	25	20	11	25	16	11	11	16	10					25	20
Tom TUNSTALL (Honda)	283	9	13	7	10		13	16	16	13	16	11	16	16	10	11	11	10	13	11	16	13	13	9	10
Chris BURNS (MV Agusta)	267	20		20	16	25						16	25			16	25	16	20	16		25		11	16
Leon MORRIS (Ducati)	165	8	10	16	7		10	13	11	16	13			13		8	10					11	10		9
Shannon ETHERIDGE (Kawasaki)	134								10		10				11	10	10	9	11		13	10	11	16	13
Michael HOWARTH (Honda)	127	6	9		8	13	11	11	9					11	8	9	13	9	10						
Malcolm ASHLEY (Kawasaki)	75	13	16	11	9							10												8	8
Luke QUIGLEY (Suzuki)	73	7		13	10	20			13																
Dan STEWART (Honda)	58													13	13							16	16		
James BUCKINGHAM (Honda)	42	11	11	9	11																				
Steve MERCER (Yamaha)	41	16		25																					
Francis WILLIAMSON (Ducati)	27														9							9	9		
Kenny GILBERTSON (Kawasaki)	11																			11					
Victor COX (Yamaha)	10																							10	
Brian McCORMACK (Honda)	8		8																						

2008 British Superbike Manufacturers Championship

Points after final round

Name	Total	R3	R4	R5	R6	R1	R2	R7	R8	R9	R10	R11	R12	R13	R14	R15	R16	R17	R18	R19	R20	R21	R22	R23	R24
Ducati	527	25	20	25	25	25	20	25	25	25	25	25	25	16	16	20	20	16	16	25	13	25	20	25	25
Honda	492	20	25	20	25	16	20	20	20	13	16	20	16	20	20	16	25	25	25	20	25	20	20	20	20
Suzuki	355	10	11	11	13	20	13	16	10	16	10	13	13	25	25	25	13	20	20	16	20	7	16	10	2
Yamaha	200	8	1	1	9	7		9	9	8	8	9	11	11	10	9	16	9	10	8	8	11	11	8	9
Kawasaki	152	7	10	6	11	9	9	5	5	5	5	10	6	8	8	4	7	4	8	3	3	8	7	4	
MV Agusta	21					2						1	3			1	6					3			5

2008 Fuchs-Silkolene British Supersport Championship

Points after final round

Round columns (one race per round): Thruxton, Oulton Park (03), Brands Hatch GP (1a), Donington Park (04), Snetterton (05), Mallory Park (06), Oulton Park (07), Knockhill (08), Cadwell Park (09), Croft (10), Silverstone (11), Brands Hatch Indy (12).

Name	Total	Thruxton	Oulton (03)	Brands GP	Donington	Snetterton	Mallory	Oulton (07)	Knockhill	Cadwell	Croft	Silverstone	Brands Indy
Glen RICHARDS	240	20	25	20	20	20	11	25	16	20	25	13	25
Hudson KENNAUGH	187	13	20	25		13	25	20	11	13	16	25	6
Ian LOWRY	146	11	16		25	11	16	16	25	8		10	8
J WESTMORELAND	136	1	5	13	6	16	10	10	20	11	20	11	13
Steve PLATER	106					25	20		25		16	20	
Chris MARTIN	99	16	13		11	8		13	8	7	7	9	7
James WEBB	87		3		10	10		8	11	13	16	13	3
Steve BROGAN	85	25	11	16	13	10				5	5		
Paul YOUNG	68	7		6	7			7		10	11	20	
Rob FROST	63	5			9		7	5	8	9	9		11
Daniel COOPER	50		9	5			7	9		2	1	8	9
Marty NUTT	49		9	8	2	6	6				10	5	3
Craig FITZPATRICK	46	3	8	10	8	2		3			5	2	5
Ian HUTCHINSON	42	8	7	9				13	5				
BJ TOAL	42		10	11	5	5	9				2		
Joe DICKINSON	31			4		1	4	4		3	8	7	
Steven NEATE	27	6	6	3			1	2	6			1	2
Jack KENNEDY	24								10	1	6	6	1
Andy WEYMOUTH	19		4	7		4				1	3		
Miguel PRAIA	16				16								
Sam OWENS	16					3	3		6	4			
Josh BROOKES	16												16
Ben WYLIE	13			2	4			7					
Tom GRANT	10	10											
Ashley BEECH	10				1	9							
John McGUINNESS	10								2	4	4		
Pete SPALDING	9										9		
Aaron WALKER	7		4					2	1				
Tommy BRIDEWELL	6									6			
Dean HIPWELL	5			1									4
Alastair SEELEY	4											4	
Midge SMART	3		2	1									
Ross WALTER	3						3						
Dan LINFOOT	3										3		
James HILLIER	2		2										

2008 Metzeler National Superstock 1000 Championship
Points after final round

Name	Total	Thruxton 20 April 2008	Oulton Park 5 May 2008	Brands Hatch GP 11 May 2008	Donington Park 26 May 2008	Snetterton 15 June 2008	Oulton Park - R1 20 July 2008	Oulton Park - R2 20 July 2008	Knockhill 10 August 2008	Cadwell Park 25 August 2008	Croft 14 September 2008	Silverstone 28 September 2008	Brands Hatch Indy 12 October 2008
Steve BROGAN	273	25	25	25	20	25	25	20	25	25	13	20	25
Jon KIRKHAM	215	20	20	20			20	20	25	20	20	25	25
Peter HICKMAN	125	11	9		8	10	11	8	3	16	16	13	20
Alistair SEELEY	108	9	13	13	13	16		10	7		11		16
Ben WILSON	103		11		9	9	5	9		11	20	16	13
Adrian COATES	102			9	16	13	13	16	1	13	10		11
Marshall NEILL	93	13	10	16	25	11			9	4	5		
Lee JACKSON	93	5	7	10	6	7	16	13		7	8	8	6
Victor COX	75	6	6	8	10	3	10	7			7	10	8
Jimmy STORRAR	56		5	11	11				11		9	4	5
Daniel HEGARTY	55		4	6	5	6			13	9		3	9
Conor CUMMINS	53	10	16			4	7	5				7	4
Kenny GILBERTSON	52		8				8	4	16	10	6		
Cameron DONALD	44	16					9	6	8	5			
Howie MAINWARING	39	7			7	8		11				6	
Sam WARREN	35				4	2	3	3	10		4	9	
Dan STEWART	23	2	3	5			6	2			3	2	
Richard COOPER	21											11	10
Kieran BLAIR	13		2	7			1				3		
Steve MERCER	11						2				2		7
Kieran CLARKE	11								1	6	2		2
Alex CAMIER	10	1			3	5						1	
Ian HUTCHINSON	9										8	1	
Peter WARD	9	4			1	4							
Gary JOHNSON	8	8											
Barry BURRELL	8				2						6		
Gavin HUNT	8			3						4	1		
Martin BUCKLES	6											5	1
Adrian CLARK	5										5		
Craig BEGGS	5			4	1								
Johnathan HOWARTH	3	3											
Christian ELKIN	3												3
Phil BEVAN	2			2									
Craig McCLELLAND	2										2		
James COX	1		1										
Michael ELLIOTT	1			1									

2008 Metzeler National Superstock 600 Championship
Points after final round

Name	Total	Thruxton 20 April 2008	Oulton Park 5 May 2008	Brands Hatch GP 11 May 2008	Donington Park 26 May 2008	Snetterton 15 June 2008	Oulton Park 20 July 2008	Knockhill 10 August 2008	Cadwell Park 25 August 2008	Croft 14 September 2008	Silverstone 28 September 2008	Brands Hatch Indy - R1 12 October 2008	Brands Hatch Indy - R2 12 October 2008
Lee JOHNSTON	207	9	16	16	20	20	13	25	16	20	20	16	16
Robbie BROWN	166	8	25	11	25	13		11	13	25		10	25
Chris NORTHOVER	135	20	9		7	8	5	20	20		13	20	13
Allan Jon VENTER	132	5	20		16	16	25	9	10	7	11	4	9
Luke JONES	124	25		25	11	25			5	8	25		
Jimmy HILL	112		13			10	7	16	25		16	25	
Luke STAPLEFORD	81	6		8	5	11	20	10		6	9	2	4
Jamie HAMILTON	77	16	8	7	13	6	11		7			3	6
David HAIRE	62	11	10	13	8				1	4		7	8
Alex GAULT	59	7		9	6		10	7		10	10		
Leon HUNT	53		20			9	9					5	10
Joe BURNS	48				10	4		13		13	8		
Joshua DAY	47	10		2	9	7	16			9	2		1
Jonathan DICKSON	46	4		5				4	11	9	7	6	
Ollie LINSDELL	43			10				3	6	3	6	8	7
Matt BILTON	37					1				1	4	11	20
Nikki COATES	37	1	6	6			2	6		16			
Jess TRAYLER	36					5		4			3	13	11
Joel MORRIS	21	13					8						
Jack GROVES	20						3	5	9	2	1		
Jay DUNN	19		7	4	3					5			
Liam LYON	17							8				9	
Joe ACKROYD	16		5							11			
Michael BOOTH	13		4						4				5
Christian IDDON	11		11										
Sam NEATE	9						1		8				
Patrick McDOUGALL	8										5		3
G HOGTON-RUSLING	7			3	4								
Mike McLEAN	6						6						
Andy YELLAND	5		3		2								
Dan KNEEN	5		1			2		2					
Steve SMITH	4			1						3			
Brad HOWELL	3	3											
Johnny BLACKSHAW	3					3							
Jonathan LODGE	2	2											
Robert GUINAN	2		2										
Andrew SENNETT	2									2			
AJ JOHNSON	2												2
Jonathan RAILTON	1					1							
K MORLEY-PAYNE	1							1					
Nick CLARK	1											1	

2008 Relentless British 125GP Championship
Points after final round

Name	Total	Thruxton 20 April 2008	Oulton Park 5 May 2008	Brands Hatch GP 11 May 2008	Snetterton 15 June 2008	Mallory Park - R1 29 June 2008	Mallory Park - R2 29 June 2008	Oulton Park 20 July 2008	Knockhill 10 August 2008	Cadwell Park 25 August 2008	Croft 14 September 2008	Silverstone 28 September 2008	Brands Hatch Indy 12 October 2008
Matthew HOYLE	190	16	25	25			4	25	25	25		25	20
Tim HASTINGS	162	2	9	13	11	13	20	20	16	13	25	20	
Paul JORDAN	135	25		16	25	11	11	10	8	11	4	10	4
Tom HAYWARD	134	8	10	10	16	20	10	11		16	13	11	9
Connor BEHAN	118	5	20	8	2	16		7	6	6	16	16	16
James LODGE	109	1		7	9	7	13	9	11	5	9	13	25
Martin GLOSSOP	107	6			20			25	16	20	20		
Luke HINTON	91	9	11	20	10	10		8	9	3	6	4	1
Shaun HORSMAN	86		6	6	16		9	4	7	7	11	9	11
Jay LEWIS	71			9	8		16			10	20		8
James EAST	71		13			6	5	13	13	8			13
Lee COSTELLO	63	11	16	5	6	25							
Jordan THOMPSON	52			3	3	9	8		5	2	8	8	6
Michael WILCOX	38	20			5		7	6					
James FORD	36	13	8		7	5		1				2	
Taylor MACKENZIE	31		4			4	2	3	3			5	10
Jordan MALTON	24		3		1	8	6	2		1	3		
Niall WADDELL	23								5	10		5	3
Stewart FINLAY	21	10			11								
Catherine GREEN	20		7	4								7	2
Deane BROWN	19									9	10		
Jamie MOSSEY	11			2	4								5
Jon VINCENT	8		5			3							
Phillip WAKEFIELD	8		2			2	3					1	
Luke MOSSEY	7	7											
Michael HILL	7										7		
Corey LEWIS	7												7
Adam BLACKLOCK	6											6	
Ross CONSTABLE	5	4		1									
Dan MORETON	5					1				4			
Stuart ELWOOD	5	3									2		
Nigel PERCY	4									4			
Ross ASHMAN	3											3	
Peter SUTHERLAND	3									2	1		
Andrew POLLOCK	1		1										
Ben McCONNACHIE	1						1						
Mark HANNA	1									1			

2008 Henderson Yamaha R1 Cup
Points after final round

Name	Total	Thruxton 20 April 2008	Oulton Park 5 May 2008	Donington Park - BH Race 26 May 2008	Donington Park 26 May 2008	Snetterton 15 June 2008	Mallory Park 29 June 2008	Oulton Park 20 July 2008	Knockhill 10 August 2008	Cadwell Park 25 August 2008	Croft 14 September 2008	Silverstone 28 September 2008	Brands Hatch Indy 12 October 2008
Jon KIRKHAM	250	25	11	25	25	8	25	25	6	25	25	25	25
Ben WILSON	212		16	20	20	11	20	20	25	20	20	20	20
Sam WARREN	147	10	25	11	10	20	16		16	13		16	10
Adrian COATES	130	11		16	16	9	8	13	13	10	11	10	13
Gary MASON	121	13	13	10	13	10	10	16	20	16			
Jack KENNEDY	86	9	9	8	9	16	13	11	11				
Richard COOPER	79			7	8	25		10				13	16
Sean EMMETT	64	20	20	13	11								
Marty NUTT	63	16	10	5	6	13	11		2				
Paul SHOESMITH	47		1				4	8	8	5	8	7	6
Michael NEEVES	43		3		1	4	5	6	7	2	6	5	4
Stu WILSON	40	4	6	1	2	3	6	9	9				
Shannon ETHERIDGE	38	7	4	6	5	7	9						
James COX	32	8	8	9	7								
Robert KENNEDY	31	2				6	7					8	8
Kieran BLAIR	20											11	9
Daniel BRILL	20											9	11
Brendan CLARKE	17	3	5	4		5							
Victor COX	16										16		
Neil GARSIDE	16					2		4	3		3	2	2
Sandor BITTER	14									1	7	6	
Rod LYNN	14	5	2	3	4								
Alastair SEELEY	13										13		
Charlie BISHOP	13	1		2	3			7					
Dan HEGARTY	11									11			
Jimmy STORRAR	10								10				
Rob GUIVER	10										10		
Steve PARKIN	10										5		5
Kyle KENTISH	10								4			3	3
Connor CUMMINS	9									9			
Stephen THOMPSON	9										9		
Darren BELLWORTHY	8									8			
John INGRAM	7		7										
Mark CRINGLE	7										7		
Steve HENEGHAN	7												7
Phil BEVAN	6	6											
Scott ROWBOTTOM	6										6		
Tony RAINFORD	5							5					
Marti BROWN	5								5				
Liam MARCHANT	4										4		
Phillip CROWE	4											4	
Andrew MARRIOTT	4											4	
Yaron SALINGER	3						3						
Agoston ROSIVALL	3										3		
Pete BRADSHAW	2						2						
Steven CUSICK	1						1						

2008 Focused Events
KTM Super Duke Battle
Points after final round

Name	Total	Round 01 Thruxton 20 April 2008	Round 02 Donington Park - R1 26 May 2008	Round 03 Donington Park - R2 26 May 2008	Round 04 Snetterton - R1 15 June 2008	Round 05 Snetterton - R2 15 June 2008	Round 06 Mallory Park - R1 29 June 2008	Round 07 Mallory Park - R2 29 June 2008	Round 08 Knockhill - R1 10 August 2008	Round 09 Knockhill - R2 10 August 2008	Round 10 Cadwell Park - R1 25 August 2008	Round 11 Cadwell Park - R2 25 August 2008	Round 12 Brands Hatch Indy 12 October 2008
David WOOD	256	25	6	25	10	25	25	20	25	25	25	25	20
Kelvin REILLY	205	11	25	16	20	16	16	16	9	20	20	20	16
Ed SMITH	142		11	10	16	11	10	11	20	13	16	13	11
Dave HEAL	142	16	16	13	5	13	13	13	13	7	10	10	13
Richard COOPER	135			20	25	20	20	25					25
James EDMEADES	134	20	13	8		10	11	10	7	16	13	16	10
Jonathan PEARSON	114	10	20	11	6	9			16	11	11	11	9
Gary BYRNE	70				11		7	9	11	6	9	9	8
Paul LANE	67	9			7	6	5	8	8	9	6	7	2
Ryan LOWE	66	8	9	3	9	8	2	6	1	10	5	4	1
Stuart MacLURE	62	5	4	7			9	7	2	8	7	6	7
Pat SHAUGHNESSY	50				2	7	6	4	10		8	8	5
Nick HOBDEN	44	2	5	5	3	4	4		3	5	4	5	4
Peter HASLER	41	7	2	4	13	3			5	3		1	3
Andy DENYER	39	4	7	6	4	5	8	5					
Ryan HARRIS	34	3	10	9	8		1	3					
Luke HALL	22		8		1	1		2	6	4			
Alex GAULT	13	13											
Matt WALKER	9								4	2		3	
Simon NASH	8			1		2	3				2		
William MARSHALL	6	6											
Bruce WILSON	6												6
Tony HUGHES	5										3	2	
Steve JOY	3		3										
Colin MOULD	3			2				1					
Matthew FLYNN	3	1									1	1